My name is Brand  *there would be a true wr...* *my time have gone through. If you are finding ...... airtight container that it was meant to be placed in, you will soon realize that it was done so for a purpose. The masters/leaders of the people in the age that I lived were corrupt; they put in place our media, our schools, and our religions for the purpose of governing over our every thought and move. Almost everything that the people knew, they knew only because they allowed it. They made them think that their history was unknown; this was far from the truth.*

Almost everything that happened to these people was not only intentionally done to keep them afraid of one another, to keep them separated from one another, but also to keep them almost on the level of ignorance for the purpose of making sure that they would never be able to rise up and rule over themselves. Sadly, this went on here with almost everyone completely unaware. They lived till the day they died never knowing that this system was intentionally put into place for the purpose of controlling them and their thoughts from the very beginning.

Knowing that I would never live long enough to see the day, I wrote this so that you will be given a chance to take back what has been taken away. And in order for you to

1

do that, you will have to have the knowledge and understanding that we have purposely been kept from. You will have to break free from the thoughts that they have been programming in you, and not only realize that everyone has pieces of the puzzle, but that everyone is important, everyone matters.

It is only then that their system will break down; it is only then that the people will see the truth. With the truth, over time, you will learn to not be afraid of one another, to not be afraid to speak to one another, and to not be afraid to come to conclusions together. It is only then that the people will see that they do not need a leader, they do not need a messiah, they will be everything they never wanted you to be, free.

Best of luck,
Brandon Levon

NEW WORLD BIBLE

THE STORY OF THE TRUTH

Brandon Levon

RIVER STYX PUBLISHING CO.

TO PURCHASE THIS BOOK RETAIL OR WHOLESALE, PLEASE VISIT
THE OFFICIAL WEBSITE AT:
WWW.NEWWORLDBIBLE.ZOOMSHARE.COM

RIVER STYX PUBLISHING CO.
P.O. BOX 3246
TERRE HAUTE IN.
47803

OLDWORLDSECRETCODES@ZOOMSHARE.COM

CHAPTER 1

The Beginning

The information that you are about to obtain will change your status from having the knowledge of what mankind thinks of as a human, to having the knowledge of god!!! It is unknown when the first man arrived here on earth, but the oldest footprints were found in Kenya. An article written by Matthew Bennett, of Bournemouth University, stated: "Some 1.5 million years ago, an ancient human ancestor left this footprint on a sandy plain in eastern Africa. Scientists are celebrating the newly discovered prints as the earliest proof of upright walking. "Now we have the solid evidence for modern foot anatomy," John Harris, an anthropologist with the Koobi Fora Field School of Rutgers University, told LiveScience."

The oldest human remains were found in Ethiopia, Africa. They were three fossil skulls dated to be around 160,000 years. The oldest gold mines were the mines of Monotapa in southern Zimbabwe, South Africa. They were dated September 1988, by a team of international physicists to be around 80,000 to 115,000 years old. According to Zulu legend, these mines were worked by "artificially produced flesh and blood slaves created by the first people".

Africa is also the place known to have the oldest religion. This was discovered by Associate Professor Sheila Coulson, while studying the origin of the Sanpeople, in what is now the African nation of Botswana. There, a 70,000 year old, 19.7 foot long, 7.2 foot high, man made serpentine rock carving was found.

It was published Friday December 1, 2006 in "The Vancouver Sun" that this was done by an ancient python worshipping people. It stated, "this pushed the roots of religion back 30,000 years from its originally recorded birth place in Stone Age Europe to ancient Southern Africa in the middle of the Kalahari Desert."

This site was located within the peaks known as the Tsodilo Hills, made famous for having the largest concentration of rock paintings in the world. It is a place known by the San as "the mountains of the gods" and according to their cultures creation myth, "humans descended from the snake people who carved out ancient dry streambeds while searching the hills for water".

Now although this is one of the oldest known creation stories on earth, this same story can be found everywhere except for where the history has somehow been completely destroyed. All throughout the Middle East, there are stories of the people being created by a serpent race. In Japan, emperors say we were created by dragon gods that came from the sky, and in China the Serpent Queen Nu Kua bred with man. Australian aborigines tell stories of a reptilian race that controls man from under the earth, they believe they are descendants of dragon humans. The Warramunga called these serpents people the Wollunqua.

India also has the same tail but calls them Naga's, and claims they seeded their royal families. In Africa the serpent god Aido-Hwedo assisted in creating the world. And In South America, the Mayans taught their people that their ancestors were the people of the serpent. The Aztecs say they were created by a serpent woman. And the Hopi Indians teach that sky gods came to earth to breed with their women, they refer to them as their snake brothers. The Indian tribe Iroquois means serpents. And Sue means snakes.

The largest snake effigy in the world is thought of to have been built by the Hopi Indians at an unknown time. It is known by the Hopi as Serpent Mound and is located in Adams County, near Peebles, Ohio. This gigantic earth embankment is almost one fourth of a mile long. It is twenty feet wide, and five feet high. The Hopi call it Tokchi'I, meaning "Guardian of the East".

It is important that you understand that all of these ancient cultures have one thing in common, they contributed everything that they were, and everything that they ever were taught, to the serpent people, the Asians. They were masters of the heavens, and the stars were their road maps to any destination in the world. The calendars that they used, and passed along, were the most accurate ever known to man. One of the most well known of these, in the place that I lived, was referred to as a zodiac.

Many people were unaware of this in my time, but the planets and the stars were the source of the inspiration for their modern day calendars, and clocks of twelve numbers. Still to this day, the clocks had to be reset so that they could be aligned to the movement of the planets. Over time, this knowledge of the heavens allowed this ancient race of people to predict almost every event in the sky and on earth. When a flood or tragic event would happen, stars were picked out of the skies based on the alignments of the planets. These would then not only represent the time of the event, but the time that the event was expected to reoccur in the future. I guess the easiest way to explain the zodiac would be this; it is the story of creation and the events that surround it.

To give you an ideal of what one of these calendars actually looks like, it was made by drawing a circle representing a year. You then divide the circle into 12 separate parts, each one known as an age, house, or mansion. These twelve were then divided into four by a cross through a sun in the center. This then represented the suns travel throughout the year, the winter solstice to the summer solstice, and then the spring, the autumnal equinox to the vernal equinox.

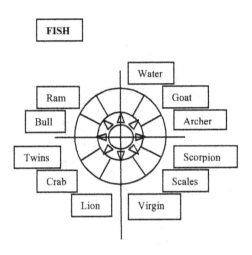

This is an example of a zodiac; we are in the age of the fish. This depiction is the representation of a cycle that at the time of the writing of this book lasted approximately 26,000 years. It was known as the precession of the equinoxes. This cycle was caused by the earth's unequal distribution around its rotational axis, this caused it to wobble. When the sun was measured against the fixed stars, this wobble caused it to end up in a slightly earlier position at the time of the spring equinox each year. This was called precession, as opposed to progression, because the movement slipped backwards through the zodiac. In precession, the ages moved from Virgin, to Lion, to Crab, so on and so forth, all the way back to the beginning, with each age lasting approximately two thousand years.

Above is a rough depiction of the Hopi sun symbol; it is not only their symbol for this ancient zodiac cycle, but it is also the Hopi representation of their story of creation. This story has been verbally passed along, from generation to generation, since the beginning of time, handed down in poem and song, as instructed by their creator. Each of its four rays, also known as the "cosmic cross", symbolizes each

10

of the four worlds that are or were subject to a global disaster.

According to Hopi tradition, they say that Tokpela was the name of the first world; they say that it was perfect. They say that the reason why the people were created for this first world was to form a perfect union between heaven and earth. They claim that at the time of its creation, the people were made with their hearts in tune with Taiowa and the earth. Taiowa was known as the creator, and sadly, almost all of the people who walked the earth in the time that I lived, were unaware that these stories represented actual dates in time. The date, or age, in which this story is referring to on the zodiac, is the age of the goat, the age of the creator.

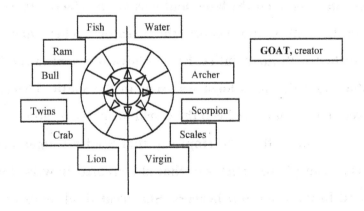

The Hopi say that in the time of the creator, Taiowa made Sotuknang, his nephew, and ordered him to make this world. They say that at first this world had the land, water, and air. They say that Sotuknang then created a helper and he called her Kokyangwuti (spider woman). When Spider woman asked why she was here, Sotuknang told her that it was to help create this world.

She then took some earth, mixed it with some saliva, and molded it into two beings. She covered them with a white substance cape, and when she uncovered them, the two beings asked her, "why are we here". She said to the one on the right, you are Poqanghoya; you are here to help keep the world in balance when life is put upon it. Then she told him to go around the world and make sure it was fully solidified.

She then told the twin on the left, you are Palongawhoya, and you are here to help keep the world in balance when life is put upon it. He was also responsible for putting sound on the land, and was often referred to as echo, because all sound echoes the creator. When they were finished with their duties, Poqanghoya was sent to the North Pole, and Palongawhoya was sent to the south. There, they were commanded to keep the world properly rotating.

After this, the Hopi say that Spider women created trees and plants. They say that she created flowers, bushes, seed bearers and nut bearers. She created all kinds of birds and animals, molding them out of the earth, bringing them to life with her white substance cape. The Hopi claim that the first people were told to spread out to all corners of the earth

12

to live. They say that at that time not only did all of the people understand each other, but they understood the world that they lived on.

They say that the people were pure and happy, and that the most important things on the planet were the big headed snake, and the fat eating bird. They say that at this time, the people and the animals could understand each other without talking; they felt as one, all living together in harmony as they multiplied upon the face of the earth. The Hopi claim that they remained that way until around the time that would be indicated on the zodiac as the beginning of the age of the archer, the age of the savior.

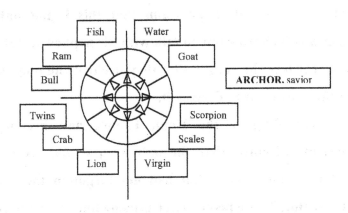

The Hopi claim that it was around this time that Lavaihoya came along; he was known as the talker. The Hopi say he came as a bird; he convinced the people that they were not only different from the animals, but that the people were different from each other. He led them away from their wisdom and they began to see themselves as being different colors, they began to speak different languages, and started having different beliefs in what the creator had told them. It was at this time that the animals began to stay away from the people, and the people began to stay away from each other.

The Hopi say that it was because of this that they began to separate into groups, all of the people of different races and languages, those that remembered the story of the creator, and those that did not. They say that the people were in constant dispute, always at battle; they say that they became fierce and warlike, and that this made Taiowa, the creator, very upset. They claim that this is not only the reason why Taiowa came to talk with his nephew Sotuknang, but that it was the reason that they decided the only way to save the world was to destroy it.

According to the Hopi, Taiowa and his nephew, Sotuknang, decided that the only people that were to be saved were the people that had not forgotten the story of their creator. These people later became known as the chosen people; they were given that name because they were saved from the coming destruction. The Hopi say that these chosen people were instructed to follow a certain cloud by day, and a certain star by night. They say that these people were told to not take anything with them, and that the journey that they were about to take would not end until the star and cloud stopped.

It is important to note that most of the people in the time that I lived were unaware of the fact that every star had a role that it played as it crossed the night sky, each one appearing and disappearing out of site at different times, on different days of the year. These stories were told so the people would be able to find their way, sung so they would not forget the story of the stars, the story of the creator. When a star appears in the sky, any number of people from any given direction can follow it, and with very little knowledge, no matter where they are in the world, they will all end up at the same destination.

According to the Hopi, it was at this time that all over the world these people just picked up and started following this star and cloud, a star and cloud that only the chosen people were able to locate. They claim that most of the other people just laughed at them because they could not see the star. The Hopi say that this was because they had lost their inner wisdom; they had forgotten the story of the creator.

When the last of the chosen people arrived to their destination, they say that Sotuknang led them to a mound where the ant people lived. They claim that he stomped on

15

the roof and demanded that the ant people open their home. When they did, Sotuknang then told the people to go in, and that they would be safe in their when he destroyed the first world. He told them that they needed to learn a lesson from the ant people. He told them that "the ant people were industrious; they gather food in the summer and store it for the winter, they keep cool when it is hot and warm when it is cool. They live peacefully with one another and they obey the plan of creation".

After the people were safe inside, Taiowa commanded Sotuknang to destroy the world. The Hopi say that Sotuknang destroyed it by fire because the fire Clan had been the world's leader. They claim that he opened up all of the volcanoes, and that fire not only came up from below, but showered down from above as well. They say that fire came from everywhere until the earth and the waters were all one element, fire. This is said to have continued until there was nothing left except for the people who were safe inside the womb of the earth. After they emerged, they claim that Sotuknang had put land where the water had been and water where the land once was. They say that Sotuknang told them that this was done so that this wicked world would not be remembered in any way, so that Tokpela, the first world, would be no more.

Oddly, and although widely challenged, a guy named Ed Conrad claimed he found evidence of a similar nature. He stated "Physical evidence currently exists that proves man inhabited the earth while coal was being formed, shaking the very foundations of who we really are and how we really got here. An assortment of human bones and soft organs, transformed to rock-like hardness, has been discovered between anthracite veins in Pennsylvania. Since one of the golden rules of geology is that coal was formed during the Carboniferous -- a minimum of 280 million years ago -- it means that man has existed multi-millions of years before the ... insectivore from whom the evolutionists claim we eventually evolved. However, the scientific establishment has wielded its powerful disdainful influence -- deceit, dishonesty, collusion and conspiracy -- to prevent evidence of the most important discovery of the 20th century to be documented as fact and, therefore, keep us from learning a monumental truth about ourselves."

No matter whether these bones are real or not, this story from the Hopi dates to the age of the scorpion, the age of the destroyer. The destroyer is the end of the first world that the Hopi lived in. It is their first story of creation, from the beginning to the end, and when we take all of the cultures around the world and put them all together, we get the complete story of the zodiac, the creator, the savior, and the destroyer.

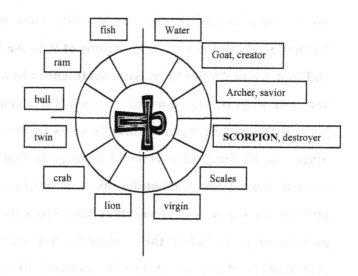

The symbol in the middle of this zodiac is much older than the cross of Christianity; this symbol is known as an Egyptian ankh, or "key of life". When it is put inside of the zodiac, it represents the same disastrous cycle that is referred to by the Hopi. In Egypt it was held only by the most knowledgeable of the gods, it represented the knowledge that they had of our future. The top of this Ankh or "key of life", in ancient times was known as the ring of shem, in my time it was known as the omega symbol. When it was in the form of the ankh, "Key of life", it represented the four great disasters that occur during this approximate 26,000 year cycle.

18

It is in the age of the destroyer, around 18,000 years ago, that many scientists now believe volcanic activity caused the sea levels to jump up to around the same levels that they are today. These discoveries match the Hopi story of creation exactly. For example, research done in the Mediterranean has led scientists to conclude that there was a 300% increase in explosive volcanic activity for this time period. These sudden eruptions are believed to be the reason for the melting of vast layers of ice around the world.

According to Dr. Peter Clark, during the time of the age of the destroyer, the ice sheets that were covering North America were over a mile higher than Mt. Hood. The top of Mt. Hood is approximately 11,000 feet, that is over two miles high. He claimed that they extended all the way from the west coast of Canada, east to New England. Scientists refer to this as the Laurentide ice sheet because of the Laurentain Mountains that this ice sheet engulfed.

Other evidence was found in core samples that were extracted from deep within the Greenland ice sheet. These samples verified that at this time there was an increase in the numbers of volcanic dust and sulphate layers due to eruptions across the northern hemisphere. The scientists who conducted these studies claim that the amount of volcanic activity at this time was so great in this area alone that it could have affected the entire planet. They claim that just before this disaster, there were hundreds of thousands of cubic miles of ice stacked up on many of the continents as glaciers. They say that after these volcanic eruptions, there was a change in the coastlines by at least 1 mile. These changes are said to have caused land bridges all around the world.

For example, it is said that Alaska was connected by land bridge with eastern Siberia. This is the land bridge that many scientists believe humans used to migrate to North America; they refer to it as "Beringia" or "Bering land bridge". They say that Mainland Australia was connected to both New Guinea and Tasmania and that the British Isles were an extension of continental Europe because of the dry bed of the English Channel. It is even believed to have dried up the basin of the South China Sea, linking Sumatra, Java and Borneo to the Asian mainland.

Another example can be found in a group of eight caves and rock shelters located in Lake County Oregon. Discoveries there led researchers to the conclusion that they were underwater up until the water levels dropped around 17000 to 18000 years ago, the age of the destroyer. Before then, the evidence indicated that the present rock outcroppings in the desert of the Summer Lake Basin, in Oregon, were nothing more than islands.

Now despite the fact that there was physical evidence to prove that this happened, the Hopi were not the only ones with this story. The Mayan calendar was based on the same cycle. Their texts claim that for every one of these four worlds, the gods were making a new race of people. Their version of creation says that the first world consisted of plants and living beings, but because they were unable to pay homage to the gods, they were destroyed.

There stories were interwoven with the movement of the stars giving reference to the time that they occurred. Plato stated in his dialogues about this type of writing, he stated: "there have been, and will be again, many destructions of mankind...brought about by the agencies of fire and water...once upon a time Phaethon, the son of Helios, having yoked the steeds in his father's chariot, because he was not able to drive them in the path of his father, burnt up all that was upon the earth, and was himself destroyed by a thunderbolt. Now this has the form of a myth, but really signifies a declaration of the bodies moving in the heavens around the earth, and a great conflagration of things upon the earth, which recurs after long intervals."

Chapter 2

The New World

According to the Hopi, the chosen people survived this cataclysmic event, which occurred during the time of the age of the destroyer, by living underground with the ant people, eating their food, and learning their industrious ways. They claim that they remained underground until the earth had cooled enough for them to once again start to repopulate and restore balance. It is at this time that the people began again in the second world. The second world was known to the Hopi as Tokpa, and this balance began again in the age of the creator, the age of the scale.

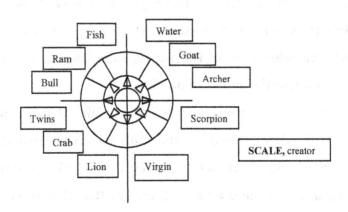

When Sotuknang first showed up in the age of the creator to speak to the chosen people, the Hopi say that he first spoke to the ant people; they say that he thanked them for doing their part in saving the chosen people. He told them that what they had done would always be remembered, and that there would come a day when this new world would be destroyed once again. He told them that when that day comes, "all of the evil people on it will know that their last day on earth is here". He said that "they will one day sit by the ant hills and cry for the ants to save them".

Sotuknang told the people that emerged onto this new surface that they should always "consider the ant" he told them to study and remember the ants' efficient ways. He told them to multiply and be happy, to keep the world in balance, "never forget the creator and the laws he has given them". According to the Hopi, the people then spread out in all different directions, they say that at this time, they could reach the other side of the world, matching exactly to the modern scientific studies of my day.

It is at this time that the Hopi claim that the people were still able to remember the skills they had learned from the first world. They say that they could still communicate telepathically amongst each other, but that they were never able to communicate telepathically with the animals again. The Hopi claim that this second world was not quite as

24

beautiful as the first one. But even so, they still spread out and multiplied in greater numbers than they had before. They claim that they lived the entire time of the creator in happiness, by gathering only what they needed to survive, and nothing more. By the time that is represented by the age of the savior, the Virgin, they say that the people had covered the world.

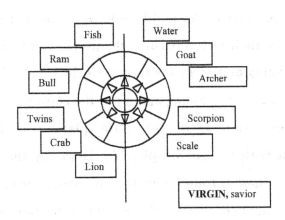

The Hopi claim that at this time, they had everything that they needed; they say that they had built homes and villages, with trails in between them. They made beautiful objects, and traded them with each other. According to their story of creation, despite all of the good, of this entire world, over time it was just not enough and they began to trade for things that they did not need. They say that the more goods they were able to get their hands on, the more goods they wanted. They say without even realizing it, many of them began to forget the story of the creator. The Hopi say that it was all of these things combined that led to the people fighting once again.

They say it led many of them to only care about the goods that they were able to get and store. And that over time many of them quit singing the songs of the creator, causing Sotuknang, the savior, to appear before them. The spider clan was their leader and he told them that because of their evil ways, their web was running out. He told them that Taiowa was going to destroy the second world.

Taiowa and Sotuknang again put the chosen people in a safe place. And again this safe place was hiding underground with the ant people. The Hopi say that after they were safe underground with the ant people, Sotuknang commanded the twins Poqanghoya and Palongawhoya to leave their posts at the north and south ends of the world's axis, preventing it from properly rotating. They say that this set the world off balance and that the world spun around crazily and rolled over twice. They claim that all over the world the water came up over the lands and the mountains plummeted into the seas. The Hopi claim that because the world was spinning out of control when the water went up over the land, it caused it to freeze into solid ice. The time that this is dated to is the age of the Lion, once again the age known as the destroyer.

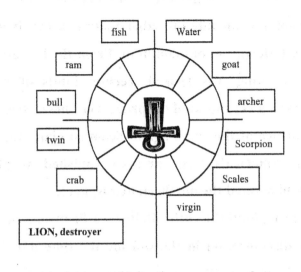

The age of the Lion/destroyer is one of the most well researched times in earth's history. Most researchers agree that at this time, dust storms in Asian deserts sent tons of sediment into the air while Glaciers grew across the tops of mountains in the northern hemisphere. They believe that the forests of northern Europe were turned into frozen tundra while the area around Delaware, Maryland, and Virginia, now known as the Delmarva Peninsula, became uninhabitable.

This period in time is known as the last great ice age, it is referred to as the Younger Dryas. It was named that after an arctic flower that flourished around that time.

The catastrophe that occurred during this age caused so much destruction to the earth that at least 30 known recorded species of animals suddenly became extinct. Some of these animals include the saber tooth cat, the dyer wolf, and almost all species of mammoth. From the biggest to the smallest, nothing was spared, certain kinds of rabbits, skunks, even a certain kind of spruce were never seen living on the surface of the earth again. Scientist claim that 80% of North America's large animals vanished as glaciers suddenly blanketed the northern hemisphere.

Throughout the entire Delmarva Peninsula there is a two foot discoloration in the soil for the time dated to be around 13,000 to 11,000 years, exactly the same time as the age of the destroyer. This has been confirmed by many Scientists and archeologists such as Darrin Lowery. He tested the soil of that period and found that at that time, the area was attacked by one of the most severe climate changes in recorded human history. It is because of this discovery that we now know that places such as Delaware, Maryland, and Virginia, were engulfed by deadly dust storms.

In places like Greenland, the scientists who have conducted core samples for this time, recovered blades of grass and pine needles. This was considered a break through in the scientific community because almost all of the present day theories were geared toward claiming that

28

this process took place over thousands of years. It is because of this study that it is now known that this would have been scientifically impossible because there would have been no way for there to have been thriving plant life found frozen in place. They concluded that there was no other way for this to have happened unless it had happened very quickly.

One of the most well know people to dig ice core samples for this period in time was Dr. Ed Brooks, from Oregon state university, he dug ice cores from both Greenland and Antarctica. According to him, because of the fact that when ice freezes, it traps little bubbles of air inside of it, he was able to cut ice cores dating to around thirteen thousand years, and melt them to recover the air bubbles for testing. By doing this, he was able to determine what conditions were like. He was surprise to find that at that time there was a sudden wide spread climate change throughout the world. They were able to conclude that it was not just places like Maryland and Virginia, but that much of the world had gone through a catastrophic event.

Discoveries like this have led many scientists to believe there was a pole shift, matching exactly to the description of events claimed by the Hopi. Scientists believe that at this time the North Pole was somewhere north of where the state of Wisconsin is and that the South Pole was in the Pacific Ocean. This was further confirmed by animal and plant life found frozen in Antarctica. One of which is the extinct species of mammoth which was said to have went extinct during this time period. It was found frozen in place with forms of plant remains still in its mouth. Discoveries like these have led scientists to conclude that this is the time when the ice cap was formed there. At the present time it is widely believed that before this cataclysmic event, Antarctica was a tropical place.

In fact, the evidence for a pole shift occurring in this time period was so great that years before these discoveries, in 1958, Charles Hapgood presented 458 references to prove that the earth had shifted on its axis several times in the past. He claimed the last one could have been as little as 11,600 years ago, not far from modern scientific belief. Charles Hapgood was a member of what is now known as the CIA, he had access to more knowledge than most of us ever did. It is interesting to note that sometime after his attempt to inform the public, he was accidentally hit by a car.

Other evidence supporting this event can be found in the oldest human remains ever discovered in the Americas. These remains were dated to 13,000 years ago, the beginning of the age of the destroyer. Scientists claim that the skull found belonged to a 26 year old woman who died by the edge of a gigantic prehistoric lake during the time of the last ice age, this location is now occupied by the suburbs of Mexico City.

Scientist from Liverpool's John Moores University and Oxford's research Laboratories of Archeology are the ones that determined the date. It is 2000 years older than the next oldest to be found, again, the exact same time as the age of the destroyer. The skull that was found was long and narrow and is said to be Caucasian in appearance, it resembled the skulls of the white western Europeans who lived in the time I wrote this book.

The projectile points that have been found for the time period of the skull are referred to as Clovis. After the Younger Dryas, the age of the destroyer, no evidence of Clovis were found again on the Delmarva Peninsula. According to the Mayan texts the people of the second world were created out of mud, and because they forgot to pay homage to the gods (remember the story of creation), these people were destroyed. Archeological research also indicated that there was no human violence until the population expanded, also confirming what the Hopi had claimed.

Chapter 3

The Creator

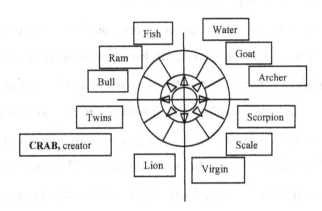

After the destruction of the second world, the Hopi say that the third was named Kuskurza. By combining the symbols and stories of these ancient calendars and cultures; we find that the third world advanced once again in the age of the creator, the beginning of the age of the crab. The Hopi say that this third world was created after Sotuknang ordered the twins, Poqanghoya and Palongawhoya, back to their position.

They say that after they returned, the earth began to thaw. This then revealed that Sotuknang had once again rearranged the water and the land. They say that he again put the land where the water used to be, and the water where the land had once been. He put on this new world new rivers and new mountains to make certain that the previous world would all but be erased to everyone except the chosen people, they were to leave a marker of this event, reminding them to always remember the story of the creator.

Now this is one of the most important points of their story because we know they actually built these markers due to astrologically aligned structures such as the sphinx. Researchers who have studied the sphinx believe that it was built when Egypt was still a fertile grass land due to the evidence of erosion that has been found on it. This evidence suggests that it had to have been built before the younger Dryas because of the fact that there has been no steady rainfall in Egypt since before the time of 10,000 BC.

When Graham Hancock, the author of "The Message of the Sphinx", ran a computer program on this structure, it was found that the sphinx only looked up at itself in the constellation of Leo on one date, 10,500 BC, the time of the age of the destroyer.

This is not by any chance some type of random coincidence; the sphinx had the body of a lion and the head of a virgin. This is the exact same time represented on the zodiac as the cross of the savior. The people who would have been part of the organization that was responsible for the building of this sphinx would have known that they were to take cover when the alignment of this structure was about to occur.

In fact once you begin to learn the true history of mankind, one has to wonder if when people like Edgar Cayce claimed that there was a lost library of ancient knowledge stored under the sphinx, if he may have had some kind of inside information. Kind of like a joke that was being played on the unsuspecting herd of mankind.

The new human beings that would emerge after the end of the Clovis people, in the age of the creator, are known as Folsom people. They were named that after Folsom New Mexico, were evidence of their tools were first discovered. These Folsom people are said to be the ones who over the next few thousand years populate the new world.

According to the researchers of this time period, these people are the same race of people that meet Christopher Columbus in the 15th century. They say that there mix is part Asian and part Caucasian, and that there race is the race of the Indians that lived in America when I wrote this book. These Indians were said to have settled at their location around 10,000 years ago, the age of the crab, the age of the creator. According to the Hopi, this was around the same time that Sotuknang told the chosen people that they could emerge from the ground. The Hopi say that they then climbed up from the home of the ant people by using a ladder, and that after this, the people began to spread out and multiply on the lands once again.

They say that in the first world, the people were in tune with the animals. In the second world, they had advanced to building homes and villages. And in the third world, with the knowledge that the chosen people had from the first two, they were multiplying and advancing even quicker than they had ever done before.

It is in this third world that the Hopi speak of a female that was known to them as a great prostitute. In the beginning of the modern bible, there is a reference to who she was. When you translate the words of the Old Testament back to the original Hebrew, the words can have many meanings. When done to genesis 1:1 the creation of the earth took place millions of years before Genesis 1:2 which states: "now the earth had been devastated, and in waste; and the presence of death was in the deep. Ruwach of the Elohim hovered above the surface of the waters."

When you translate back to the original Hebrew, genesis 3:8, it states: "and they heard the voice of the lord god (as he was) walking in the garden with Ruwach that day." These are the only two times that Ruwach is mentioned in the bible and she was known by many names such as queen of heaven, queen of wisdom, wisdom, Sophia, goddess of virginity, goddess of war, Athene, and the Christians

36

referred to her as the Holy Spirit. The father the son and the Holy Spirit, she was what we would consider today to be Roman or Greek.

It is during this age that the Hopi say that Athena had many men wrapped around her finger. They say that she began to become known throughout the world for her wickedness and corruption of so many people. They claim that so many men had given her turquoise necklaces for her favors that she could wind them around a ladder that could reach the end of the world's axis. They claim that this wicked woman convinced many men to use their creative powers for evil and that this material girl led mankind down the path of great destruction and a terrible world war.

Athena is one of the people responsible for the cult of women that was referred to as the Amazons. They were a nation of all female warriors. Hippocrates described them stating: "They have no right breasts... for while they are yet babies their mothers make red-hot a bronze instrument constructed for this very purpose and apply it to the right breast and cauterize it, so that its growth is arrested, and all its strength and bulk are diverted to the right shoulder and right arm." They not only believed that women were superior over men, but they were partly to blame for what would later become the slave race.

It is in the beginning of this third world, not long after the destruction of the second, that her seeding of nations can be dated in Plato's dialogs when he states: "She founded your city a thousand years before ours... the seed of your race...afterwards she founded ours... ...eight thousand years old... if you compare these very laws with ours you will find that many of ours are the counterparts of yours as they were in the olden times. In the first place there is the caste of priests... artificers... shepherds... hunters... husbandmen... weapons... shields and spears... goddess taught of Asiatic first to us, as in your part of the world first to you. Then as to wisdom... our law... made a study of the whole order of things... prophecy... medicine... health... all this order and arrangement the goddess first imparted to you when establishing your city...wherefore the (goddess), who was a lover both (of war) and (of wisdom), selected and first of all settled that spot which was the most likely to produce men likest herself...as became the children and disciples of the gods..."

Plato wrote this some time around 360 BC as happened 9000 years before. That's 9360 plus the 2000 years that have passed, making the seeding of their race approximately 11,360 years ago. This means that her seed started this race of people just after the end of the second world, around the end of the age of the lion, just after the time that was represented by the sphinx.

Plato refers to Athena many times in his dialogues, and describes how for every language her name is pronounced different, he states: "in the Egyptian delta...the city which king Amasis came. The citizens have a deity for their foundress; she is called in the Egyptian tongue Neith, and is asserted by them to be the same whom the Hellenes call Athene... ...and are in some way related to them."

In Plato's Critias, he states, "Now different gods had their allotments in different places which they set in order. Hephaestus and Athene, who were brother and sister, and sprang from the same father... obtained as their common portion this land... and put into their minds the order of government..." it goes on to tell the story in the same manner as the Hopi in speaking of the people forgetting the story of the creator when it states: "but the virtues and the laws of their predecessors, they knew only by obscure traditions; and as they themselves and their children lacked for many generations the necessaries of life, they directed their attention to the supply of their wants, and of them they conversed, to the neglect of events that had happened in times long past."

Athena was known as the virgin patron of Athens. To the Greeks her father was known as Zeus and to the

Romans he was called Jupiter, on his head he wore a crown with horns. The father of Zeus was named Kronos; Kronos was usually depicted as a bent old man with a sickle in one hand and a serpent that bites its own tail in the other. This serpent biting its own tail was the representation of this cycle of the zodiac; it is the story of how the earth creates and then eats its own children. (See world book encyclopedia)

Kronos had three sons, Zeus, Poseidon, and Hades, according to Plato's dialogs there was no fighting in this new world until after the time of Athena. Plato states: "In the days of old, the gods had the whole earth distributed among them by allotment. There was no quarrelling... They all of them by just apportionment obtained what they wanted, and peopled their own districts; and when they had peopled them they tended us, their nurslings and possessions, as shepherds tend their flocks, excepting only that they did not use blows or bodily force, as shepherds do, but governed us like pilots from the stern of the vessel, which is an easy way of guiding animals, holding our souls by the rudder of persuasion according to their own pleasure; thus did they guide all mortal creatures."

These three sons of Kronos are the gods that control the world at this time. They were a white race and they seeded almost all of our nations. It is because of there ability

40

to preserve/save knowledge during the time of the savior, just before these great destructions that makes them the most technologically advanced people on the face of the earth, they were the gods, they were the creators of the new worlds.

According to Plato, it is around this time that Poseidon/EA starts the building of a place in the Atlantic Ocean we now call Atlantis. Plato talks about this stating: "in speaking of the allotments of the gods..." (The three sons of Kronos: Poseidon, Hades and Zeus.) "they distributed the whole earth into portions differing in extent, and made for themselves temples and instituted sacrifices. And Poseidon, receiving for his lot the island of Atlantis, begat children by a mortal woman, and settled them in a part of the island, which I will describe. Looking towards the sea, but in the centre of the whole island, there was a plain which is said to have been the fairest of all plains and very fertile."

"Near the plain again, and also in the centre of the island at a distance of about fifty stadia, there was a mountain not very high on any side. In this mountain there dwelt one of the earth-born primeval men of that country, whose name was Evenor, and he had a wife named Leucippe, and they had an only daughter who was called Cleito. The maiden had already reached womanhood, when her father and mother died; Poseidon fell in love with her and had intercourse with her, and breaking the ground, enclosed the

41

hill in which she dwelt all round, making alternate zones of sea and land larger and smaller, encircling one another; there were two of land and three of water, which he turned as with a lathe, each having its circumference equidistant every way from the centre, so that no man could get to the island, for ships and voyages were not as yet."

"He himself, being a god, found no difficulty in making special arrangements for the centre island, bringing up two springs of water from beneath the earth, one of warm water and the other of cold, and making every variety of food to spring up abundantly from the soil. He also begat and brought up five pairs of twin male children; and dividing the island of Atlantis into ten portions, he gave to the first-born of the eldest pair his mother's dwelling and the surrounding allotment, which was the largest and best, and made him king over the rest; the others he made princes, and gave them rule over many men, and a large territory. And he named them all; the eldest, who was the first king, he named Atlas, and after him the whole island and the ocean were called Atlantic."

"To his twin brother, who was born after him, and obtained as his lot the extremity of the island towards the pillars of Heracles, facing the country which is now called the region of Gades in that part of the world, he gave the name which in the Hellenic language is Eumelus, in the language of the country which is named after him, Gadeirus. Of the second pair of twins he called one Ampheres, and the other Evaemon. To the elder of the third pair of twins he gave the name Mneseus, and Autochthon to the one who followed him. Of the fourth pair of twins he called the elder Elasippus, and the younger Mestor. And of the fifth pair he gave to the elder the name of Azaes, and to the younger that of Diaprepes."

"All these and their descendants for many generations were the inhabitants and rulers of divers islands in the open sea; and also, as has been already said, they held sway in our direction over the country within the pillars as far as Egypt and Tyrrhenia. Now Atlas had a numerous and honourable family, and they retained the kingdom, the eldest son handing it on to his eldest for many generations; and they had such an amount of wealth as was never before possessed by kings and potentates, and is not likely ever to be again, and they were furnished with everything which they needed, both in the city and country. For because of the greatness of their empire many things were brought to them from foreign countries, and the island itself provided most of what was required by them for the uses of life."

"In the first place, they dug out of the earth whatever was to be found there, solid as well as fusile, and that which is now only a name and was then something more than a name, orichalcum, was dug out of the earth in many parts of the island, being more precious in those days than anything except gold. There was an abundance of wood for carpenter's work, and sufficient maintenance for tame and wild animals. Moreover, there were a great number of elephants in the island; for as there was provision for all other sorts of animals, both for those which live in lakes and marshes and rivers, and also for those which live in mountains and on plains, so there was for the animal which is the largest and most voracious of all."

"Also whatever fragrant things there now are in the earth, whether roots, or herbage, or woods, or essences which distil from fruit and flower, grew and thrived in that land; also the fruit which admits of cultivation, both the dry sort, which is given us for nourishment and any other which we use for food—we call them all by the common name of pulse, and the fruits having a hard rind, affording drinks and meats and ointments, and good store of chestnuts and the like, which furnish pleasure and amusement, and are fruits which spoil with keeping, and the pleasant kinds of dessert, with which we console ourselves after dinner, when we are tired of eating, all these that sacred island which then beheld the light of the sun, brought forth fair and wondrous and in infinite abundance. With such blessings the earth freely furnished them; meanwhile they went on constructing their temples and palaces and harbors and docks. And they arranged the whole country in the following manner."

"First of all they bridged over the zones of sea which surrounded the ancient metropolis, making a road to and from the royal palace. And at the very beginning they built the palace in the habitation of the god and of their ancestors, which they continued to ornament in successive generations, every king surpassing the one who went before him to the utmost of his power, until they made the building a marvel to behold for size and for beauty."

"And beginning from the sea they bored a canal of three hundred feet in width and one hundred feet in depth and fifty stadia in length, which they carried through to the outermost zone, making a passage from the sea up to this, which became a harbor, and leaving an opening sufficient to enable the largest vessels to find ingress. Moreover, they divided at the bridges the zones of land which parted the zones of sea, leaving room for a single trireme to pass out of one zone into another, and they covered over the channels so as to leave a way underneath for the ships; for the banks were raised considerably above the water."

"Now the largest of the zones into which a passage was cut from the sea was three stadia in breadth, and the zone of land which came next of equal breadth; but the next two zones, the one of water, the other of land, were two

45

stadia, and the one which surrounded the central island was a stadium only in width. The island in which the palace was situated had a diameter of five stadia. All this including the zones and the bridge, which was the sixth part of a stadium in width, they surrounded by a stone wall on every side, placing towers and gates on the bridges where the sea passed in."

"The stone which was used in the work they quarried from underneath the centre island, and from underneath the zones, on the outer as well as the inner side. One kind was white, another black, and a third red, and as they quarried, they at the same time hollowed out double docks, having roofs formed out of the native rock. Some of their buildings were simple, but in others they put together different stones, varying the colour to please the eye, and to be a natural source of delight."

"The entire circuit of the wall, which went round the outermost zone, they covered with a coating of brass, and the circuit of the next wall they coated with tin, and the third, which encompassed the citadel, flashed with the red light of orichalcum. The palaces in the interior of the citadel were constructed on this wise: In the centre was a holy temple dedicated to Cleito and Poseidon, which remained inaccessible, and was surrounded by an enclosure of gold; this was the spot where the family of the ten princes first saw

46

the light, and thither the people annually brought the fruits of the earth in their season from all the ten portions, to be an offering to each of the ten."

"Here was Poseidon's own temple which was a stadium in length, and half a stadium in width, and of a proportionate height, having a strange barbaric appearance. All the outside of the temple, with the exception of the pinnacles, they covered with silver, and the pinnacles with gold. In the interior of the temple the roof was of ivory, curiously wrought everywhere with gold and silver and orichalcum; and all the other parts, the walls and pillars and floor, they coated with orichalcum."

"In the temple they placed statues of gold: there was the god himself standing in a chariot—the charioteer of six winged horses—and of such a size that he touched the roof of the building with his head; around him there were a hundred Nereids riding on dolphins, for such was thought to be the number of them by the men of those days. There were also in the interior of the temple other images which had been dedicated by private persons. And around the temple on the outside were placed statues of gold of all the descendants of the ten kings and of their wives, and there were many other great offerings of kings and of private persons, coming both from the city itself and from the foreign cities over which they held sway. There was an altar too, which in size and workmanship corresponded to this magnificence, and the palaces, in like manner, answered to the greatness of the kingdom and the glory of the temple."

"In the next place, they had fountains, one of cold and another of hot water, in gracious plenty flowing; and they were wonderfully adapted for use by reason of the pleasantness and excellence of their waters. They constructed buildings about them and planted suitable trees, also they made cisterns, some open to the heaven, others roofed over, to be used in winter as warm baths; there were the kings' baths, and the baths of private persons, which were kept apart; and there were separate baths for women, and for horses and cattle, and to each of them they gave as much adornment as was suitable."

"Of the water which ran off they carried some to the grove of Poseidon, where were growing all manner of trees of wonderful height and beauty, owing to the excellence of the soil, while the remainder was conveyed by aqueducts along the bridges to the outer circles; and there were many temples built and dedicated to many gods; also gardens and places of exercise, some for men, and others for horses in both of the two islands formed by the zones; and in the centre of the larger of the two there was set apart a race-course of a stadium in width, and in length allowed to extend all round the island, for horses to race in."

"Also there were guard-houses at intervals for the guards, the more trusted of whom were appointed to keep watch in the lesser zone, which was nearer the Acropolis; while the most trusted of all had houses given them within the citadel, near the persons of the kings. The docks were full of triremes and naval stores, and all things were quite ready for use. Enough of the plan of the royal palace."

"Leaving the palace and passing out across the three harbors, you came to a wall which began at the sea and went all round: this was everywhere distant fifty stadia from the largest zone or harbor, and enclosed the whole, the ends meeting at the mouth of the channel which led to the sea. The entire area was densely crowded with habitations; and the canal and the largest of the harbors were full of vessels and merchants coming from all parts, who, from their numbers, kept up a multitudinous sound of human voices, and din and clatter of all sorts night and day."

"I have described the city and the environs of the ancient palace nearly in the words of Solon, and now I must endeavor to represent to you the nature and arrangement of the rest of the land. The whole country was said by him to be very lofty and precipitous on the side of the sea, but the country immediately about and surrounding the city was a level plain, itself surrounded by mountains which descended towards the sea; it was smooth and even, and of an oblong shape, extending in one direction three thousand stadia, but across the centre inland it was two thousand stadia. This part of the island looked towards the south, and was sheltered from the north. The surrounding mountains were celebrated for their number and size and beauty, far beyond any which still exist, having in them also many wealthy villages of country folk, and rivers, and lakes, and meadows supplying food enough for every animal, wild or tame, and much wood of various sorts, abundant for each and every kind of work."

"I will now describe the plain, as it was fashioned by nature and by the labors of many generations of kings through long ages. It was for the most part rectangular and oblong, and where falling out of the straight line followed the circular ditch. The depth, and width, and length of this ditch were incredible, and gave the impression that a work of such extent, in addition to so many others, could never have been artificial... It was excavated to the depth of a hundred feet, and its breadth was a stadium everywhere; it was carried round the whole of the plain, and was ten thousand stadia in length. It received the streams which came down from the mountains, and winding round the plain and meeting at the city, was there let off into the sea."

"Further inland, likewise, straight canals of a hundred feet in width were cut from it through the plain, and again let off into the ditch leading to the sea: these canals were at intervals of a hundred stadia, and by them they brought down the wood from the mountains to the city, and conveyed the fruits of the earth in ships, cutting transverse passages from one canal into another, and to the city. Twice in the year they gathered the fruits of the earth—in winter having the benefit of the rains of heaven, and in summer the water which the land supplied by introducing streams from the canals."

"As to the population, each of the lots in the plain had to find a leader for the men who were fit for military service, and the size of a lot was a square of ten stadia each way, and the total number of all the lots was sixty thousand. And of the inhabitants of the mountains and of the rest of the country there was also a vast multitude, which was distributed among the lots and had leaders assigned to them according to their districts and villages."

"The leader was required to furnish for the war the sixth portion of a war-chariot, so as to make up a total of ten thousand chariots; also two horses and riders for them, and a pair of chariot-horses without a seat, accompanied by a horseman who could fight on foot carrying a small shield, and having a charioteer who stood behind the man-at-arms to guide the two horses; also, he was bound to furnish two heavy-armed soldiers, two archers, two slingers, three stone-shooters and three javelin-men, who were light-armed, and four sailors to make up the complement of twelve hundred ships. Such was the military order of the royal city, the order of the other nine governments varied, and it would be wearisome to recount their several differences."

"As to offices and honours, the following was the arrangement from the first. Each of the ten kings in his own division and in his own city had the absolute control of the citizens, and, in most cases, of the laws, punishing and slaying whomsoever he would. Now the order of precedence among them and their mutual relations were regulated by the commands of Poseidon which the law had handed down. These were inscribed by the first kings on a pillar of orichalcum, which was situated in the middle of the island, at the temple of Poseidon, whither the kings were gathered together every fifth and every sixth year alternately, thus giving equal honour to the odd and to the even number."

"And when they were gathered together they consulted about their common interests, and enquired if any one had transgressed in anything, and passed judgment, and before they passed judgment they gave their pledges to one another on this wise:--There were bulls who had the range of the temple of Poseidon; and the ten kings, being left alone in the temple, after they had offered prayers to the god that they might capture the victim which was acceptable to him, hunted the bulls, without weapons, but with staves and nooses; and the bull which they caught they led up to the pillar and cut its throat over the top of it so that the blood fell upon the sacred inscription."

"Now on the pillar, besides the laws, there was inscribed an oath invoking mighty curses on the disobedient. When therefore, after slaying the bull in the accustomed manner, they had burnt its limbs, they filled a bowl of wine and cast in a clot of blood for each of them; the rest of the victim they put in the fire, after having purified the column all round. Then they drew from the bowl in golden cups, and pouring a libation on the fire, they swore that they would judge according to the laws on the pillar, and would punish him who in any point had already transgressed them, and that for the future they would not, if they could help, offend against the writing on the pillar, and would neither command others, nor obey any ruler who commanded them, to act otherwise than according to the laws of their father Poseidon."

"This was the prayer which each of them offered up for himself and for his descendants, at the same time drinking and dedicating the cup out of which he drank in the temple of the god; and after they had supped and satisfied their needs, when darkness came on, and the fire about the sacrifice was cool, all of them put on most beautiful azure robes, and, sitting on the ground, at night, over the embers of the sacrifices by which they had sworn, and extinguishing all the fire about the temple, they received and gave judgment, if any of them had an accusation to bring against any one; and when they had given judgment, at daybreak they wrote down their sentences on a golden tablet, and dedicated it together with their robes to be a memorial."

"There were many special laws affecting the several kings inscribed about the temples, but the most important was the following: They were not to take up arms against one another, and they were all to come to the rescue if any one in any of their cities attempted to overthrow the royal house; like their ancestors, they were to deliberate in common about war and other matters, giving the supremacy to the descendants of Atlas. And the king was not to have the power of life and death over any of his kinsmen unless he had the assent of the majority of the ten."

"Such was the vast power which the god settled in the lost island of Atlantis; and this he afterwards directed against our land for the following reasons, as tradition tells: For many generations, as long as the divine nature lasted in them, they were obedient to the laws, and well-affectioned towards the god, whose seed they were; for they possessed true and in every way great spirits, uniting gentleness with wisdom in the various chances of life, and in their intercourse with one another. They despised everything but virtue, caring little for their present state of life, and thinking lightly of the possession of gold and other property, which seemed only a burden to them; neither were they intoxicated by luxury; nor did wealth deprive them of their self-control."

It is interesting to note that the Piri Reis map created in 1513 by 16th century Ottoman-Turkish admiral and cartographer Piri Reis, indicates that there was knowledge of these previous worlds. Along with showing part of the western coasts of Europe, North Africa, Brazil and the continent of Antarctica free of ice, it also shows various Atlantic islands such as the Azores, Canary, and the mythical island of Antillia. The island of Antillia was known by many names such as the Isle of Seven Cities, Ilha das Sete Cidade, Septe Cidades, Sanbrandan or St Brendan, the Isles of the Blest and the Fortunate Islands.

If we look back on some of these ancient maps, Antillia first shows up in the Pizzigano Chart of 1424. In fact it appears in almost all of the surviving Portolan charts of the Atlantic, the Genoese B. Beccario or Beccaria of 1435, the Venetian Andrea Bianco of 1436 and Grazioso Benincasa of 1476 and 1482. On these maps, it was drawn almost as a perfect rectangle, just like the description of Atlantis. They even show the bays as they are getting larger, as the years go by, as if they were being dug out into the large river mouths that were described by Plato. The Piri Reis map was said to be copied from several other maps including the "lost map of Columbus". Columbus was funded by the Roman Catholic Church, the descendants of the god Zeus.

"Manly P. Hall claimed that the Atlantians devised a plan – a Great Plan – which would guide world events for millennia to come, and that it included a mysterious blueprint of what would later become America. Hall said that ancient Egyptian secret societies inherited this great plan and were well aware of the existence of the land mass in the western hemisphere which we now call America, long before it was discovered by Columbus." William T. Still

Winston Churchill, 33rd Degree Freemason once stated: "The one who cannot see that on Earth a big endeavor is taking place, an important plan, on which realization we are allowed to collaborate as faithful servants, certainly has to be blind."

According to the oldest India--n myths, the first humans emerged from a golden egg laid by the king of the gods. Mark Twain once stated: "India is the cradle of the race, the birthplace of human speech, the mother of history, the grandmother of legend, and the great grandmother of tradition." Almost all none African people on the earth in the time that I wrote this book could trace their descent back to India. It is because of this that India was commonly known as mother India. Researchers of the time concluded that the rise of cities started there around 9000 years ago with the development of large villages in the Indus valley.

The first discoveries of these cities were made in 1921 at a place known as Harappa. By 1922, British and Indian archeologists uncovered an untouched site to the south known as Mohenjodaro, by ancient standard, these were considered urban giants. Their territories stretched from the Himalayas to the Arabian Sea and contained over 2000 towns and villages. They are believed to have been the largest civilizations in the ancient world with a population of somewhere around 5 million people. The language that these ancient people spoke is still undeciphered to this day, but the evidence that was found there indicated that they did a lot of trading with Persia and Iraq.

If we look into the history of Iraq, we find the Sumerian tablets; in the Sumerian language they call the father of Zeus, Anu instead of Kronos. These tablets say that Anu set up a mission to bring back gold and other precious metals. They state that this mission was first led by his oldest son Ea (house on water). He was also called Enki, which meant lord of earth; Ea was known by the Greeks as Poseidon and the Romans called him Neptune, he was the oldest son of Kronos and half brother to Zeus/Enlil. This first mission was set up at Eridu, which meant house remotely constructed. It was located close to the northwest end of the Persian Gulf, where the Tigris and Euphrates River meet the gulf. There the tablets say that they started collecting gold from the sea water.

They say that after Ea/Poseidon did not bring back as much gold and other precious metals as expected, a larger expedition was sent out commanded by Enlil/Zeus. Their plan was to set up another colony in southern Africa, known as Abzu, and then send that gold back to Mesopotamia, and from there to their home. According to the Sumerian stories, the gold expedition was set up with 900 people. There were 600 searching for gold and 300 looking after the colonies and doing the shipping. This later led to what would become known as the great pyramids of Egypt.

After searching for precious metals by means of hard labor, the people in southern Africa rebelled and it was suggested creating a worker which could do the work instead. According to the Sumerian tablets, after the approval of this slave race, Ea's half sister Ninki, also known as Nin-khursag, or "lady of life", carried the first worker to term and then gave birth, they called it the Lulu. After this they decided to use fourteen goddesses to make more Lulu workers.

The Sumerian tablets refer to the place where they put one of the first Lulu/slaves as Edin, he was to watch over the tablet of destiny. This was also indicated in the modern bible when it refers to this first Lulu as Adam in the Garden of Eden watching over the tree of knowledge. It is because of these Sumerian tablets that we not only know what this tree of knowledge actually was, but that there were also many people, gods, etc., living on the earth when Adam was born.

Genesis 4:13 states: "Cain replied to the Lord, (Enlil) my punishment is greater than I can bear. (14) For you have banished me from my farm and from you, and made me a fugitive and a tramp; and everyone who sees me will try to kill me. (15) The lord (Enlil) replied, they won't kill you, for I will give seven times your punishment to anyone who does. Then the Lord (Enlil) put an identifying mark on Cain as a warning not to kill him." This mark was his brand, his social security number. It is the mark that has always been given to their cattle/Herd.

Webster's New World Dictionary, Herd: "(1) a number of cattle or other large animals feeding or living together (2) a crowd (3) the common people; masses." Remember, Plato's dialogues states that the gods: "governed us like pilots from the stern of the vessel, which is an easy way of guiding animals, holding our souls by the rudder of persuasion according to their own pleasure; thus did they guide all mortal creatures."

When Poseidon took for himself a mortal wife, he broke the covenant of his elders. He was giving to the people who were born on the surface of the earth, the knowledge of the gods. Plato stated: "And Poseidon, receiving for his lot the island of Atlantis, begat children by a mortal woman." And he wanted to raise his children and their ancestors to be like him. Genesis 1:27 "so god made man like his maker. Like god did god make man; man and maid did he make them."

According to the Sumerian tablets, the revealing of the secrets of the elders to his children led to the decision that Ea was to be banned from the Garden of Eden. Ea rebelled against this decision and secretly started an organization known as the "Brotherhood of the Serpent". The serpent was the ancient symbol for knowledge. This symbol was not only the symbol of Ea, but it was also the symbol of his father Anu; it was passed on to Ea because he was the first born son.

The fact is, the writers of the modern bible were the first cult ever in the recorded history of man to represent the serpent as evil. Genesis chapter 3 states, "The serpent was the craftiest of all the creatures the lord god (EA) had made. So the serpent (EA) came to the woman. "Really?" he asked. "None of the fruit in the garden? God (Enlil) says you mustn't eat any of it." (2, 3) "Of course we may eat it," the

60

woman told him. "It's only the fruit from the tree at the center of the garden (tablet of destiny) that we are not to eat. God (Enlil) says we mustn't eat it or even touch it, or we will die." (4) "That's a lie!" the serpent (EA) hissed. "You'll not die! (5) God (Enlil) knows very well that the instant you eat (study) it you will become like him, for your eyes will be opened."

What is so important about this age is not only the fact that it is the time of the first ever recorded secret society, but it is also the first time that we can actually prove that someone was breeding, and assigning to their offspring, gods to represent every ages of the zodiac. For example, the creator god of India, in the age of the Crab, was known as Brahma, he is one of the Hindu trinity; the other two are Vishnu and Shiva. Brahma is the creator, Vishnu or Krishna is the preserver or savior, and Shiva is the destroyer. In the Hindu story of creation, Brahma created the fathers of the human race. He is usually depicted with four heads, four faces, and four arms; they are the representation of the four arms of the cross of the zodiac. It is no coincidence that Jyotisha, the Hindu system of astrology, is the corner stone of western astrology.

Chapter 4

The Savior

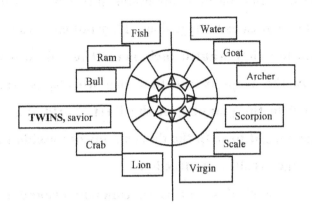

By the time of the age of the twins, the savior, Atlantis was a metropolis. It made Harappa in India look like a small village and according to the Sumerian tablets, the knowledge to build such cities was handed down from before the time that the gods had walked the surface of the earth, recorded in what was known by them as the tablet of destiny. The tablet of destiny was handed down to the two brothers, Enlil/Zeus and Ea/Poseidon by their father, Anu/Kronos. They then handed the tablets down to their eldest sons, with each generation that followed doing the same. It is during this age, that tribe of Zeus bred another slave race; this race is also referred to as Adam. In fact the

63

word Adam to these people seems to be a word that is given to the first born of every new race that they breed.

This type of conduct was not practiced by the descendants of Poseidon; they were free to do as they pleased and they had no need for material things. This led the descendants of Zeus to be jealous. They not only wanted their wealth, but they wanted their land. These desires as described by the Hopi in the first two worlds, is what eventually led to the planning of the First World War, a war that was fought to strip the descendants of Poseidon of their knowledge, wealth, and freedom.

The story of this war is so common around the world that there is a version of it almost everywhere you go. One of the most well known of this story is actually referred to as the two brothers, one holds a sword to fight for good, and the other holds a sword to fight for evil. In places like India they were known as the "Awains", Romans "twin brethren", and in China, "yin and yang". This story is also found in Babylon, Arabia, and is marked in the Bible in the story of the Garden of Eden. It is the reason why the twins/ cherubim represent this age of the zodiac. Genesis 3:24, "so he drove out the man; and he placed at the east of the garden of Eden cherubim's, and a flaming sword which turned everyway, to keep the way of the tree of life."

This war was started by using the knowledge of flight; they flew in and attacked their own city. The ideal was to make the people think that the cult of Poseidon had done so unprovoked. The key to the truth behind this attack is the fact that the ancestors of Poseidon are the Hopi, and they never cared about wealth. After the descendants of Zeus won this war, he became known as the lord of the air.

His symbols became birds, the main one the eagle, and his messengers were depicted with wings. This attack turned the people against Ea/Poseidon; it convinced them that his descendants were evil. It is because of this war that the people began to call Ea/Poseidon lord of vermin and prince of demons. It is because of this war that the modern bible referred to Ea as the serpent. It is because of this war that almost all of the people that walked the earth in the time that I lived did not have a clue of what the "tree of life" actually was.

After this war, all of the descendants of Anu/Kronos that had taken on mortal wives became known as the fallen angels, for disobeying the laws of the new god Zeus. The people of my time actually thought that the word angel referred to something good, it did not. They were the warriors and messengers of the descendants of Zeus. They were the ones who were helping out with the plan of killing/sacrificing the descendants of Ea and erasing from the face of the earth the story of creation for the purpose of keeping their status as gods. Whether the followers of this god knew throughout time or not, they worshiped the god who wanted to keep mankind in the dark, they worshiped the true prince of Darkness, Lucifer, Zeus.

Manly P. Hall, 33rd degree mason once stated: "I hereby promise the Great Spirit Lucifer, Prince of Demons, that each year I will bring unto him a human soul to do with as it may please him, and in return Lucifer promises to bestow upon me the treasures of the Earth and fulfill my every desire for the length of my natural life. If I fail to bring him each year the offering specified above, then my own soul shall be forfeit to him."

Both the Masonic and Satanic symbol was the five pointed star, the symbol of Athena and her mother. This symbol was usually represented with the goat. The goat was the symbol of the first age of the first world of the zodiac. The satanic bible was written by Anton LaVey who was once a member of this Masonic order, which is why their rituals are so similar. My wife was once a high priestess in a satanic grotto and spent time at Anton's house when he was still alive. Now although she no longer practiced Satanism when I wrote this book, Anton stated that "he withdrew himself from the Masonic order because he could not stand to be around such evil people". The question is, if these people

66

came from outside of our solar system, why would they randomly pick the symbol of Venus to represent them?

In the book of Enoch, found in Ethiopia in 1786, the place were the new slaves were bred from, there is a list of the people that wanted us to be like the gods, a list of the fallen angels, it states: "Samyaza, Arakiba, Rameel, kokabiel, Tamiel, Ramiel, Danel, Ezeqeel, Baraqijal, Asael, Armaros, Batarel, Ananel, Zaqiel, Samsapeel, Satarel, Turel, Jomjael, Sariel. (8) These are their chiefs of tens"

In another part of the book of Enoch it describes the things that these fallen angels were trying to teach the people who were born on the surface of the earth when it states: Chapter 8:1 "And Azazel taught men to make swords, and knives, and shields, and breastplates, and made known to them the metals of the earth and the art of working them, and bracelets, and ornaments, and the use of antimony, and the beautifying of the eyelids, and all kinds of costly stones, and all (2) colouring tinctures."

It goes on to say that "Semjaza taught enchantments, and root-cuttings, 'Armaros the resolving of enchantments, Baraqijal taught astrology, Kokabel the constellations, Ezeqeel the knowledge of the clouds, Araqiel the signs of the earth, Shamsiel the signs of the sun, and Sariel the course of the moon......Thou seest what Azazel hath done... revealed the eternal secrets which were preserved in heaven, which (7) men were striving to learn: And Semjaza, to whom Thou hast given authority to bear rule over his associates. And they have gone to the daughters of men upon the earth, and have slept with the (9) women, and have defiled themselves, and revealed to them all kinds of sins." It is no accident that this book was not included in the modern bible, these things are what made these people gods. The knowledge of these things gave these so called gods complete control over the life and death of the earth born people.

We know this because of all of the pre-flood tablets and stories of these areas. It is because of them that we were not only able to find out what it is that exactly happened around this time, but just exactly who these gods were. It is because of the tracing back of all of the stories and all of the territories mentioned and dated in things such as the book of Enoch that we now refer to these people as Aryans, an all white race of people that worshiped the stars.

In 1786, the British orientalist William Jones introduced the ideal that all languages descended from a common source. In the 1800s the philologist Max Mueller gave this proto language a name; he called it Aryan, a main language that is believed to have been used by various peoples living in the vicinity of Persia, modern Iran.

The first worship of the god that is referred to as Zeus can be traced back to the Aryans who can be traced from

Rome to Greece, to Iran, Afghanistan and India, all on the same path, the same path that produced all of the main modern religions. In India, the earliest scriptures in the world can be found, they are known as the Vedas. These stories were orally transmitted throughout the ages in poetic song like form that has kept them preserved, just like the story of the Hopi, and the telling of them to remember the story of creation.

The oldest of these scriptures is a collection of 1000 hymns known as the Rig-Veda. They are believed by scholars to have been first written down around 1500 BC. The earliest hymns in the Rig-Veda mention places in the North West, where the Aryans are first found inside the subcontinent. They settled in the valley of the Indus, the river that gave India its name, and they fought battles on a river which flowed down from Afghanistan. They herded their cattle on the river swat, which today is in Pakistan's northwest frontier, and according to the Rig-Veda; it is believed that the heart of the early Aryan territory was the region of Peshawa, in Pakistan.

The remembering of these stories was of great importance because in India, in the Indus civilization, horses were not known. In the Rig-Veda, they are a key part of the stories which talk of many wheeled chariots and horses. They tell of them bringing the gods, and tell the story of how they migrated eastwards toward the afghan border. According to the people of India, they were known as "the civilized" because they brought with them new technology, the building of cities and governments.

By tracing back the stories of the Rig-Veda, a Russian archeologist by the name of Victor Sarianidi was able to locate in the black dessert, the route that these Aryans/gods traveled out of central Asia. This then led him to the discovery of a lost civilization that at the time in which it was inhabited, was a fertile oasis. The culture that he found was the mirror image of the Aryan described in the Rig-Veda. In the kings' mausoleum were four wheeled vehicles, exactly matching the description of the carts that the people of India claim the gods were riding in. These people had casts of priests and performed fire rituals at special altars.

German researchers and scholars claim that these people were a tall blond, long headed people, that today we would call Nordic. And they claim that these people can also be traced from the shore of the Baltic Sea to south Russia. Their description matches exactly to the oldest human remains found in the Americas, the ones that belonged to the 26 year old woman who died during the Younger Dryas by the edge of the gigantic prehistoric lake.

In the Rig-Veda, it tells a tale of tribes moving across northern India, led by the god of fire, burning forests and looking for new lands. The leaders of these tribes spoke Sanskrit, and the Rig-Veda says that at this time they were battling amongst themselves, matching the story of the Sumerians and the Hopi, etc, etc, etc. It matches the story of Zeus and Poseidon.

The Rig-Veda says that they battled day and night without sleep by drinking a drink they call soma. The drink was said to be sacred to the Aryan rituals. It is said to be made from a plant with a long stock and no leaves, with a very bitter taste and a smell slightly like pine. The Rig-Veda states that they sweetened its bitter taste by using honey. The ingredient are said to be Poppy, cannabis, and ephedrine. According to the Rig-Veda, when the right amount is taken, it enlivens the senses, sharpens you up, and keeps you awake.

Not only do many of the poets of the Rig-Veda compose there songs at night after the consumption of soma, but the king of the gods was said to have drank massive amounts of this drink. It is interesting to note that the plant used to make this drink does not exist in India; it was brought from somewhere else. There are many poems in the Rig-Veda that are devoted to the king of the gods and the consumption of soma as they battled, burning the history of mankind.

It is because of this that the majority of the people of my time failed to see the connection with these people. They

71

failed to see that on the other side of the world, these stories matched the stories of the Hopi exactly. For example, according to the Hopi, by the time of the age of the savior, they had multiplied in such numbers and advanced so rapidly that they had created large cities, countries, even entire civilizations. Over time they say that this led most of them to forget their promise to the creator. The Hopi say that very few remembered, most of the people were too occupied with their earthly plans, and the ones that did remember were concerned that the others were using their reproductive powers in wicked ways. (Descendants of Zeus)

The Hopi claim that the people who were abusing their sexual powers built large glittering cities of light, each highly centralized. They say that their creator did not intend for the people to do this because he wanted them to live close to the land. They claim that the people built what they call a patuwvota and that they used their creative powers to make it fly through the air. The Hopi say that they flew this patuwvota to a big city, attacked it, and returned so fast no one knew where they came from, this is the part of the story were the descendants of Ea/Poseidon were blamed. The Hopi say that it wasn't long after this that many people in many cities built patuwvota and flew them to attack one another.

If we go back to the stories of the people of India, they claim that at this time there are at least four different

72

types of these craft. One was said to be a double decked circular aircraft with portholes and a dome. They claim that this one flew with the speed of the wind and gave forth a melodious sound. Another one is described as a long cylinder, basically shaped like a cigar. The tales of these ships are so numerous there are way too many to mention, some of them contain entire flight manuals. The most common of these ships is known as a Vimana. The word Vimana was derived from the word Vamana which means "he who is able at three strides to take measure of the entire earth and heavens."

The two Major Sanskrit epics of India are known as the Ramayana and Mahabharata. The reason for this is the fact that they were handed down verbally in poem and song for thousands of years, just like the story of the Hopi. Along with the Ramayana and Mahabharata there are numerous other ancient Indian texts that speak of a horrible war that took place with the people of the Rama Empire. The Rama Empire is one of the most well known of ancient legends in India and is said to be a nation of many large sophisticated cities. Its seven greatest capital cities were known as "The Seven Rishi Cities". According to ancient Indian text, "they battled a great nation with their Vimanas". In these Indian texts, these Aryans were known

73

as the "Asvins", and they claim that they had more technology than they did.

The weapons that were said to be used were thought of as having to be fictional up until my time, now many weapons are very similar. The Mahabharata tells of the awesome destructiveness of the war that they were in, it states: "a blazing missile of smokeless fire" is unleashed by the hero Adwattan. "Dense arrows of flame, like a great shower, issued forth upon creation, encompassing the enemy....A thick gloom swiftly settled upon the Pandava hosts. All points of the compass were lost in darkness. Fierce winds began to blow. Clouds roared upward, showering dust and gravel. "Birds croaked madly...the very elements seemed disturbed. The sun seemed to waver in the heavens. The earth shook, scorched by the terrible violent heat of this weapon. Elephants burst into flame and ran to and fro in a frenzy...over a vast area, other animals crumpled to the ground and died. From all points of the compass the arrows of flame rained continuously and fiercely."

"Gurkha, flying in his swift and powerful Vimana, hurled against the three cities of the Vrishnis and Andhakas a single projectile charged with all the power of the Universe. An incandescent column of smoke and flame as bright as the thousand suns rose in all its splendour...An iron thunderbolt, a gigantic messenger of death, which reduced to ashes the entire race of the Vrishnis and the Andhakas...." The word Andhakas was very similar to the word Anunnaki, the race that is claimed by both the bible and the Sumerian tablets to have been destroyed by the god Zeus.

It goes on to speak of them stating that "The corpses were so burned as to be unrecognizable. The hair and nails fell out; pottery broke without apparent cause, and the birds turned white....After a few hours all foodstuffs were infected.... To escape from this fire, the soldiers threw themselves in streams to wash themselves and their equipment..."

Oddly when the Rishi city of Mohenjodaro was excavated, archaeologists found skeletons lying in the street, some holding hands as if they were suddenly overtaken by some unknown force. The skeletons found there are some of the most radioactive ever found anywhere in the world, testing very close to the ones found at Hiroshima and Nagasaki, after the dropping of an Atomic bomb. There were places in India where the brick and stone walls have actually been fused together. Other places where there have been similar discoveries found include Ireland, Scotland, France, and Turkey.

The Texts found at Mohenjodaro in Pakistan, thought to be one of the Seven Rishi Cities of the Rama Empire, still remain undeciphered to this day. This writing has been found only in one other place in the world and that is Easter Island, it is called Rongorongo writing. Unfortunately no one knows what they were trying to say, because when the followers of the descendants of Zeus, the catholic missionaries, landed on this island, they burned almost all of the text that were found while converting the natives.

The Mahabharata states: "The cruel Salva had come mounted on the Saubha chariot that can go anywhere, and from it he killed many valiant Vrishni youths and evilly devastated all the city parks." another part states, "His Saubha clung to the sky at a league's length...He threw at me rockets, missiles, spears, spikes, battle-axes, three-bladed javelins, flame-throwers, without pausing....The sky...seemed to hold a hundred suns, a hundred moons...and a hundred myriad stars. Neither day nor night could be made out, or the points of compass."

Later, when Saubha becomes invisible, Krishna, the savior of the age of the twins states: "I quickly laid on an arrow, which killed by seeking out sound, to kill them...All the Danavas who had been screeching lay dead, killed by the blazing sunlike arrows that were triggered by sound."

Another ancient text known as the Mausola Purva speaks of yet another type of weapon, it states: "Cuka, flying on board a high-powered Vimana, hurled on to the triple city a single projectile charged with all the power of the universe. An incandescent column of smoke and flame, as bright as ten thousand suns, rose in all the splendor... When the vimana returned to Earth, it looked like a splendid block of antimony resting on the ground."

Here is a story from the Ramayana which indicates where one of these flying machines can be found, it states: "The Puspaka Car, that resembles the sun and belongs to my brother, was brought by the powerful Ravan; that aerial and excellent car, going everywhere at will, is ready for thee. That car, resembling a bright cloud in the sky, is in the city of Lanka."

According to the ancient Indian text known as the Samar, Vimanas were "iron machines, well-knit and smooth, with a charge of mercury that shot out of the back in the form of a roaring flame." Another work known as the Samarangana Sutradhara tells of how these vehicles were actually built.

The fact is, many texts around the world suggest that not only was there flight in ancient times, but that it was well known. Ko Hung (A.D. 283-343) once stated: "Some use the inner part of the jujube tree to make a flying vehicle, using ox leather straps fastened to encircling blades, so as to propel this machine. Some others have the idea of making five snakes, six dragons, and three oxen to encounter the hard wind, and so ride it.... In the Tai Qing region, the air is very hard, and can lift people. The Master says that a yuan flying, spiraling higher and higher, only needs to straighten out its two wings and not flap them any more to move forward, because it is riding on the hard wind."

After countless hours of research into these ancient planes, this includes many texts that are not written here, the first ones appear to be a rather simple design. They appear to have been made of a light weight frame, possibly sticks. The frame was then wrapped with a light weight animal skin or paper made from a tree. This was then painted in a bright metallic paint that shinned as it glided in the sky. These gliders were later equipped with some kind of container of liquid.

Mercury was then slowly combined in a controlled manner, causing a chemical reaction which jetted the vehicle faster. The first designs appear to be no more difficult to build than a large kite; they only went as fast as the wind would carry them. They appear to be at first launched from flattened mountain tops. The pilot could then see all that was around for many miles, he had the eyes of the eagle, the

78

definition of Vamana, "he who is able at three strides to take measure of the entire earth and heavens."

These specially designed mountains were like the train station in its time, cities grew up around them. The area of development had to have one for the leader of the city to climb and meet the pilot or god who was handing down the laws. Only the leader of the city was allowed on top, that way the pilot could safely fly in and out. If there were more than one individual, he could safely continue to the next destination. Sadly, the building of these planes were made out of material that was extremely biodegradable and in the open air, they would have disintegrated without a trace in just a few years if they were not properly maintained.

One object of interest that seemed to help prove this as fact was the Saqqara Bird, it was a plane like object made of sycamore wood. It was found in 1891 while excavating an Egyptian tomb near Saqqara. The contents of the tomb dated to at least 200 BC. This discovery was forgotten until around 80 years later when the Wright Brothers made their first landmark flight. Its resemblance to modern aircraft is so striking that a team of aviation experts assembled in the early Seventies to explore the hypothesis that it was the model of a flyable plane. After some research of the artifact, they were able to determine that the 5.6-inch long body was aerodynamically sound.

One aeronautics engineer even noted the similarity between the Saqqara Bird and a new, oblique-winged aircraft that NASA planned to build. When it was finally tested, it soared through the air like a modern-day glider. Its proportions were exact to a very advanced form of "pusher-glider". This pusher-glider was considered to be advanced because it could stay in the air at speeds as low as 45 to 65 mph, while carrying enormous payloads due to the tipping of wings downward. This unique feature is what gives both the Saqqara Bird and the pusher-glider this capability. A similar type of curving wing was implemented onto the Concorde airplane; this design gave this plane a maximum lift at a minimal speed.

Also, currently at the Smithsonian, there are a number of small South American artifacts that resemble airplanes. The smallest of these artifacts are made of gold and can not be dated although Archeologists admit they are a minimum of 1000 years old. They have been labeled as zoomorphic, meaning, animal shaped objects. An insignia found on the left side of the rudder of one of these artifacts resembles those found to mark the identification of contemporary aircraft.

In 1997, two Germans by the name of Algund Eenboom and Peter Belting, built an exact replica of one of these zoomorphic objects that was found in an Inca grave to see if it could fly. Belting made the first model with a propeller and the second with a jet engine. The first was to be launched by hand and the second was equipped with landing gear. They showed these planes at the Ancient Astronaut Society World Conference in Orlando, Florida and the propeller-powered plane flew perfectly stable. After the jet powered plan produced an impeccable take-off, flight, and landing, the crowd almost gave a standing ovation.

All of the evidence that I have been able to gather seems to supports the fact that there were places that were used as ancient runways. For example, the Nazca lines located in the dessert around 200 miles south of Lima, Peru. On a plain measuring approximately 37 miles long, and one mile wide, are etched lines and figures that were discovered in the 1930s. These lines run perfectly straight, some parallel to one another, many intersecting. The resemblance of these lines to modern runways have been mentioned in many books such as "Chariots of the Gods" written by Erich von Daniken. From the air, these lines very much resemble the ones found at the airport of area 51.

The difference is, included with these lines are carved over 70 gigantic animals of such a scale that they can only be recognized from a high altitude. Among them are a monkey, a spider, and a hummingbird, symbols that represent various ancient tribes. Once in the air, these lines pointed to the directions in which the pilot had to travel to locate them. The Indians in this area claim that the giant pictures on the ground were made by another race before the advent of the Incas.

By realizing the fact that they purposely hid from us the knowledge of flight, I would not rule out the possibility that they may have actually created all of these planes and weapons thousands to millions of years before. An article put out by the U.S. Department of Energy Office of Civilian Radioactive Waste Management stated, "It came as a great surprise to most, therefore, when, in 1972, French physicist Francis Perrin declared that nature had beaten humans to the punch by creating the world's first nuclear reactors. Indeed, he argued, nature had a two-billion-year head start. Fifteen natural fission reactors have been found in three different ore deposits at the Oklo mine in Gabon, West Africa. These are collectively known as the Oklo Fossil Reactors."

An article written in the BBC news stated, "When it set sail in December 1944, U-864 was packed with 65 tones of weapons-grade mercury destined to help the Japanese win back supremacy over the US in the Pacific - and divert American attention away from Europe in the process. Neither the cargo nor the 73 men on board made it. The U-boat was torpedoed to the bottom of the North Sea floor by a British submarine."

In the book of Enoch, found in Africa, the place where they bred the slave race, it speaks of these craft and the first time ever that they had seen the blond haired, blue eyed, light colored skin of the Aryan race that was flying them, it States, "two huge men appeared to me, the likes of which I had never seen on earth. Their faces were shinning like the sun; their eyes too, were like a burning light. And they took me up and carried me to the first heaven (city)? And they fly with their wings, and do the rounds of all the planet(s)? They led before my face the elders, the rulers of the stellar orders..." there Enoch had discussions with what he calls the most high, and they tell him about the coming destruction of the earth.

The term most high or lofty one was the term given to us to describe the rulers of our race in this age. Lofty one was later pronounced Elu in Akkadian and from it came the Babylonian, Assyrian, Hebrew, and Ugaritic, El. The word god was later given by the Greeks. The god that the people of India were assigned in the age of the twins was known as Krishna.

Krishna was the avatar of Vishnu, he was referred to as the preserver (savior). When he was born he was visited by wise men or shepherds guided by a star. The moment he was born his surroundings were splendidly illuminated. This divine one was recognized, and adored by people who prostrated themselves before this heaven-born child. He was born at a time when his foster father was away from home, having come to the city to pay his tax or yearly tribute. He was born in a state most abject and humiliating. His earthly father was a carpenter. His father was warned by a heavenly voice because the reigning monarch sought his life. The monarch ordered the massacre in all his states of all the children of the male sex born during the night of his birth. One of the first miracles he performed when mature was the curing of a leper. He cast out demons and raised the dead. He selected disciples to spread his teachings.

He was the second of the trinity. He was called the lion of his tribe, he was without sin and he celebrated a last supper. He descended into hell only to be resurrected with many people viewing his ascent into heaven. He claimed "I am the resurrection". He forgave his enemies. He is going to come again on earth and appear among mortals as an armed warrior, riding a white horse. At his approach the sun and moon will be darkened, the earth will tremble and the stars will fall from the firmament.

Krishna was the god just before the great flood story of the bible, he represented the age in which the people and their families were supposed to prepare for the events that

84

were coming on the earth in the age of the destroyer. He died on the cross of the zodiac to save the people. That is the part that almost all of the religious people of my time did not understand. They did not understand that this story was part of the tree of life; they did not understand how important it was that the god of the modern bible fought and killed to take this away from them. It did not matter who told these stories, or the laws that were interwoven for the people to follow, these stories were meant to change with the ages.

Patrizia Norelli-Bachelet, The Gnostic Circle, stated: "We also find in the RigVeda (1.154) zodiacal reference to the 3 steps of Vishnu the Preserver (whose vehicle is the Eagle) as like the Lion, the Bull and the Man. The Eagle, the Lion, the Bull, and the Man are the symbols of the four fixed (or preserving) signs, Scorpio, Leo, Taurus, and Aquarius. The mention of these signs in backward order within the zodiac, suggests that Vishnu's famous Steps correspond a movement in time - the Precession of the Equinoxes, which moves 360 degrees backward through the zodiac in 25,920 years. Vishnu's Steps have been seen by PNB to be progression in time from the Age of Scorpio (the Eagle) to the Age of Leo, to the Age of Taurus to the Age of Aquarius." From the scorpion, to the lion, to the bull, to the water.

There may have even been a code verifying these things in the bible. In genesis 5, if you add up the age of the descendants of Adam when they had their first son, Adam was 130 years old when his son Seth was born. Seth was 105 with his first son, Enosh was 90, Kenan was 70, Mahalalel was 65, Jared was 162, Enoch was 65, Methuselah was 187, Lamech was 182, and Noah was 600 years old when the flood came. $130 + 105 + 90 + 70 + 65 + 162 + 65 + 187 + 182 + 600 = 1656$, this is very close considering each age is approximately 2000 years.

If you add up the age that they lived after the birth of their first son, not including Noah, it equals 6569. Adam lived 800 years after the birth of his first son, Seth 807, Enosh 815, Kenan 840, Mahalalel 830, Jared 800, Enoch 300, Methuselah 782, Lamech 595, $= 6569$ multiplied by $4 = 26,276$. This is almost the exact number of the cycle of the zodiac, 26,000 years. Divide 26,000 by 4, you get 6,500. That means approximately every 6,500 years there is a global disaster. Adam was born out of the destruction of the age of the lion and Noah escaped the flood of the age of the bull.

Chapter 5

The Destroyer

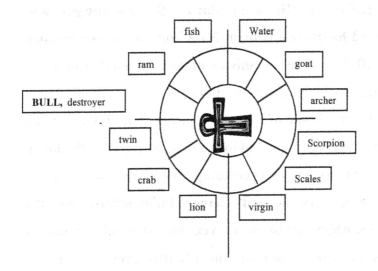

In India, in the age of the Bull, Shiva was the god of this cycle. He was the last god of the "Trimurti", or the three ages of the four worlds that represent this cycle of the zodiac. This story of the zodiac is a concept in Hinduism that represents the cosmic functions of creation, preservation, and destruction. It is personified by Brahma the creator, Vishnu or Krishna the preserver/savior and Shiva the destroyer. These three are known as the Hindu triad, or the great Trinity.

It is because of the fact that Ea wanted his descendants to have the knowledge of the gods that this part of the cycle is even remembered at all. It is because of this that Shiva is often shown garlanded with a snake. In the Shaiva tradition of Hinduism, Shiva is the supreme god, and in his hand he holds a trident. Nandi or Nandin is the name of the bull that serves as Shiva's mount. An epithet of Shiva is Pashupati, which means "lord of cattle".

In the Book of Enoch, Chapter 2:1, it tells of the signs that they told Enoch to look for to prepare for the flood, it states: "Observe ye everything that takes place in the heaven, how they do not change their orbits, and the luminaries which are in the heaven, how they all rise and set in order each in its season, and (2) transgress not against their appointed order. Behold ye the earth, and give heed to the things which take place upon it from first to last".

Chapter 10:1 states: "Then said the Most High, the Holy and Great One spake, and sent Uriel to the son of Lamech, (2) and said to him: Go to Noah and tell him in my name "Hide thyself!" and reveal to him the end that is approaching: that the whole earth will be destroyed, and a deluge is about to come (3) upon the whole earth, and will destroy all that is on it. And now instruct him that he may escape (4) and his seed may be preserved for all the generations of the world. Chapter 65: (1, 2) And in those days

88

Noah saw the earth that it had sunk down and its destruction was nigh." This is the exact same description as given for what happened to the island of Atlantis.

When Greek philosopher Plato spoke of the destruction of Atlantis, he stated: "O solon...you Hellenes are never anything but children... there is no old opinion handed down among you by ancient tradition...and I will tell you why... at such times those who live upon the mountains and in dry and lofty places are more liable to destruction than those who dwell by rivers or on the seashore..."

He goes on to later say: "Many great and wonderful deeds are recorded of your state in our histories...one of them exceeds all the rest...a mighty power which unprovoked made an expedition against the whole of Europe and Asia, and to which your city put an end. This power came forth out of the Atlantic Ocean, for in those days the Atlantic was navigable; and there was an island situated in front of the straights which are by you called the Pillars of Heracles; the island was larger than Libya and Asia put together, and was the way to other islands, and from these you might pass to the whole of the opposite continent which surrounded the true ocean; for this sea which is within the Straights of Heracles is only a harbor, having a narrow entrance, but that other is a real sea, and the surrounding land may be most truly called a boundless continent."

"Now in this island of Atlantis there was a great and wonderful empire which had rule over the whole island and several others, and over parts of the continent, and furthermore the men of Atlantis had subjected the parts of Libya within the columns of Heracles as far as Egypt, and of Europe as far as Tyrrhenia. This vast power, gathered into one, endeavored to subdue at a blow our country and yours and the whole of the region within the straights... solon, your country shown forth ...but afterwards there occurred violent earthquakes and floods; and in a single day and night of misfortune all your warlike men in a body sank into the earth, and the island of Atlantis in like manner disappeared in the depths of the sea. For which reason the sea in those parts is impassible and impenetrable, because there is a shoal of mud in the way, and this was caused by the subsidence of the island."

In Plato's Critias it states, "in comparison of what then was, there are remaining only the bones of the wasted body, as they may be called, as in the case of small islands, all the richer and softer parts of the soil having fallen away, and the mere skeleton of the land being left... For the fact is that a single night of excessive rain washed away the earth and laid bare the rock; at the same time there were earthquakes..."

It goes on later to say, "when the divine portion began to fade away, and became diluted too often and too much with the mortal admixture, and the human nature got the upper hand, they then, being unable to bear their fortune, behaved unseemly, and to him who had an eye to see grew visibly debased, for they were losing the fairest of their precious gifts; but to those who had no eye to see the true happiness, they appeared glorious and blessed at the very time when they were full of avarice and unrighteous power."

"Zeus, the god of gods, who rules according to law, and is able to see into such things, perceiving that an honourable race was in a woeful plight, and wanting to inflict punishment on them, that they might be chastened and improve, collected all the gods into their most holy habitation, which, being placed in the centre of the world, beholds all created things. And when he had called them together, he spake as follows..."

Plato just stops in mid sentence with the (descendants of the) gods in a meeting at the center of the earth, just before the great flood. We know that they are the descendants because Plato had already spoken of them as dead when he stated about the building of Atlantis, "All these and their descendants for many generations were the inhabitants". Besides that, no matter what was said during this meeting, this was the end of the reign of Poseidon's

Bloodline over their allotted part of the earth. After this disaster, Zeus became known as King of kings and god of gods over the entire allotted earth as stated in the bible, Exodus 20:3 "thou shalt have no other gods before him".

In India, the story of the saving of the chosen people was represented by "The Manu flood story". In this story, Krishna is represented as a fish. The story says that one day Manu was washing and found a fish in his water, and that the fish said, "Yes, it is me calling for your help. I need your protection," the fish told Manu, "If you take care of me, I will promise to repay you." Manu said, "You are just a small fish; from what will you save me?" the fish replied, "There will be a flood coming to wash away all the living creatures. If you help me, I will shelter you from it," Manu says to the fish, "What would you ask of me?" the fish said. "You must keep me here, away from the ocean, until I have grown. If you return me now I, will be destroyed. I am asking that you let me grow in your care until I am large enough to protect myself." So Manu told the fish, "Yes, I will care for you until you have grown." After many years growing in the care of Manu the fish told him, "Manu, you have cared for me greatly. I am now one of the largest fish and ready to return to the sea." He said "There will be a year to come in which a great deluge will occur. You must build a ship in my honor and remember me. When the flood comes, get into the ship and I will be there to save you." Manu told him, "Thank you. I will now return you to the sea."

The story says Manu did as the fish asked and built a boat and stayed near the fish. It states that after it began to rain and the waters started to rise, the fish swam toward him and Manu attached a rope to the fish and the fish pulled him toward the northern mountain. Then the fish told him, "Now you must fasten this cord to the tree and wait for the waters to recess." It says that after the waters receded, Manu realized that he was alone and that all of the creatures had been swept away. It goes on to say that after he made offerings and sacrifices to the gods, a women was produced as his daughter, and they produced all mortal races.

Manu appears in the Vedas as the performer of the first sacrifice. He is also known as the first king, and most rulers of medieval India traced their genealogy back to him, either through his son (the solar line) or his daughter (the lunar line). See Encyclopedia Britannica.

In the Epic of Gilgamesh, Gilgamesh went on a journey to find Utanapishtim. Utanapishtim was a mortal that Poseidon/Ea gave the knowledge of immortality, the tree of life, so that he and his family could live through the flood. This story not only verifies what immortality (eternal life) really means, but it verifies the time in which this happened when in Tablet 10 it states, "When Anu heard her words, he placed the nose rope of the Bull of Heaven in her hand. Ishtar led the Bull of Heaven down to the earth. When it reached Uruk It climbed down to the Euphrates... At the snort of the Bull of Heaven a huge pit opened up, and 100 Young Men of Uruk fell in. At his second snort a huge pit opened up, and 200 Young Men of Uruk fell in. At his third snort a huge pit opened up,"

It goes on to say in Tablet 10, "I have been looking at you, but your appearance is not strange--you are like me! You yourself are not different--you are like me! My mind was resolved to fight with you, (but instead?) my arm lies useless over you. Tell me, how is it that you stand in the Assembly of the Gods, and have found life!" Utanapishtim spoke to Gilgamesh, saying, "I will reveal to you, Gilgamesh, a thing that is hidden, a secret of the gods I will tell you! Shuruppak, a city that you surely know, situated on the banks of the Euphrates, that city was very old, and there were gods inside it. The hearts of the Great Gods moved them to inflict the Flood."

"Their Father Anu uttered the oath of secrecy, Valiant Enlil was their Adviser, Ninurta was their Chamberlain, Ennugi was their Minister of Canals. Ea, the Clever Prince, was under oath with them so he repeated their talk to the reed house: 'Reed house, reed house! Wall, wall! O man of Shuruppak, son of Ubartutu: Tear down the house and build a boat! Abandon wealth and seek living beings! Spurn possessions and keep alive living beings! Make all living beings go up into the boat. The boat which you are to build, its dimensions must measure equal to each other: its length must correspond to its width. Roof it over like the Apsu."

"I understood and spoke to my lord, Ea: "My lord, thus is the command which you have uttered I will heed and will do it. But what shall I answer the city, the populace, and the Elders!" Ea spoke, commanding me, his servant: "You, well then, this is what you must say to them: "It appears that Enlil is rejecting me so I cannot reside in your city, nor set foot on Enlil's earth. I will go down to the Apsu to live with my lord, Ea, and upon you he will rain down abundance, a profusion of fowl, myriad fishes. He will bring to you a harvest of wealth, in the morning he will let loaves of bread shower down, and in the evening a rain of wheat!" Just as dawn began to glow the land assembled around me the carpenter carried his hatchet, the reed worker carried his flattening stone,... the men ...""

"The child carried the pitch, the weak brought whatever else was needed. On the fifth day I laid out her exterior. It was a field in area, its walls were each 10 times 12 cubits in height, the sides of its top were of equal length, 10 times It cubits each. I laid out its interior structure and drew a picture of it. I provided it with six decks, thus dividing it into seven levels. The inside of it I divided into nine compartments. I drove plugs to keep out water in its middle part. I saw to the punting poles and laid in what was necessary."

"Three times 3,600 units of raw bitumen I poured into the bitumen kiln, three times 3,600 units of pitch ...into it, there were three times 3,600 porters of casks who carried vege- table oil, apart from the 3,600 units of oil which they consumed and two times 3,600 units of oil which the boatman stored away. I butchered oxen for the meat, and day upon day I slaughtered sheep. I gave the workmen ale, beer, oil, and wine, as if it were river water, so they could make a party like the New Year's Festival... and I set my hand to the oiling. The boat was finished by sunset."

"The launching was very difficult. They had to keep carrying a runway of poles front to back, until two-thirds of it had gone into the water. Whatever I had I loaded on it: whatever silver I had I loaded on it, whatever gold I had I loaded on it. All the living beings that I had I loaded on it, I had all my kith and kin go up into the boat, all the beasts and animals of the field and the craftsmen I had go up. Shamash had set a stated time: 'In the morning I will let loaves of bread shower down, and in the evening a rain of wheat! Go inside the boat, seal the entry!"

"That stated time had arrived. In the morning he let loaves of bread shower down, and in the evening a rain of wheat. I watched the appearance of the weather, the weather was frightful to behold! I went into the boat and sealed the entry. For the caulking of the boat, to Puzuramurri, the boatman, I gave the palace together with its contents. Just as dawn began to glow there arose from the horizon a black cloud. Adad rumbled inside of it, before him went Shullat and Hanish, heralds going over mountain and land. Erragal pulled out the mooring poles, forth went Ninurta and made the dikes overflow."

"The Anunnaki lifted up the torches, setting the land ablaze with their flare. Stunned shock over Adad's deeds overtook the heavens, and turned to blackness all that had been light. The... land shattered like a... pot. All day long the South Wind blew ..., blowing fast, submerging the mountain in water, overwhelming the people like an attack. No one could see his fellow, they could not recognize each other in the torrent. The gods were frightened by the Flood, and retreated, ascending to the heaven of Anu. The gods were cowering like dogs, crouching by the outer wall."

"Ishtar shrieked like a woman in childbirth, the sweet-voiced Mistress of the Gods wailed: 'The olden days have alas turned to clay, because I said evil things in the Assembly of the Gods! How could I say evil things in the

Assembly of the Gods, ordering a catastrophe to destroy my people!! No sooner have I given birth to my dear people than they fill the sea like so many fish!" The gods--those of the Anunnaki--were weeping with her, the gods humbly sat weeping, sobbing with grief, their lips burning, parched with thirst. Six days and seven nights came the wind and flood, the storm flattening the land. When the seventh day arrived, the storm was pounding, the flood was a war--struggling with itself like a woman writhing in labor. The sea calmed, fell still, the whirlwind and flood stopped up. I looked around all day long--quiet had set in and all the human beings had turned to clay!"

Another story of the flood is the Sumerian Ziusudra, it was found in pour condition. What can be read states, "The Flood... ...Thus was treated... Then did Nintu weep like a... The pure Inanna set up a lament for its people, Enki took counsel with himself, An, Enlil, Enki and Ninhursag..., The gods of heaven and earth uttered the name of An and Enlil. Then did Ziusudra, the king, the pashishu of..., Build a giant...; Humbly, obediently, reverently he..., ...the gods a wall... Ziusudra, standing at its side, listened. "Stand by the wall at my left side..., By the wall I will say a word to you, take my word, Give ear to my instructions..."

"...a flood will sweep over the cult centers; To destroy the seed of mankind... Is the decision, the word of the assembly of the gods. By the word commanded by An and Enlil... Its kingship, its rule... ... ..." About forty lines are missing but it goes on to talk about the flood. "All the windstorms, exceedingly powerful, attacked as one, at the same time, the flood sweeps over the cult centers. After, for seven days and seven nights, The flood had swept over the land, and the huge boat had been tossed about by the windstorms on the great waters, Utu came forth, who sheds light on heaven and earth, Ziusudra opened a window on the huge boat, The hero Utu brought his rays into the giant boat."

After this, Ziusudra, the king, prostrated himself before Utu. He kills an ox, and then slaughters a sheep. There is a break of about 39 lines and then it states, "An and Enlil uttered "breath of heaven," "breath of earth," by their ... it stretched itself, Vegetation, coming up out of the earth, rises up. Ziusudra, the king, Prostrated himself before An and Enlil. An and Enlil cherished Ziusudra, Life like a god they gave him: Breath eternal like a god they bring down for him. Then, Ziusudra, the king, The preserver of the name of vegetation and of the seed of mankind, In the land of crossing, the land of Dilmun, the place where the sun rises, they caused to dwell." Note that the king is the preserver/savior of the name of vegetation and of the seed of mankind.

According to Chibcha legends, Bochica was a bearded man who came from the east. They claim that he taught the Chibcha people civilization with one spiritual and one secular leader. They say that he taught them agriculture, metal working, and other important things. And just like the story of the Hopi, they claim that later, after they had turned to a life of excess, a flood engulfed their civilization.

The fact is, there are many stories that can be dated to the time of the great flood of the bible, more than 100 around the world. Plato even states that it is caused by water coming up from the ground when he stated, "where as in this land...water comes up from below...traditions preserved here are the most ancient". In an article written for National Geographic News February 27, 2007, by Richard A. Lovett, entitled "Huge Underground "Ocean" Found Beneath Asia", it stated, "A giant blob of water the size of the Arctic Ocean has been discovered hundreds of miles beneath eastern Asia, scientists report."

"Researchers found the underground "ocean" while scanning seismic waves as they passed through Earth's interior. But nobody will be exploring this sea by submarine. The water is locked in moisture-containing rocks 400 to 800 miles (700 to 1,400 kilometers) beneath the surface. "I've gotten all sorts of emails asking if this is the water that burst out in Noah's flood," said the leader of the research team,

Michael Wysession of Washington University in St. Louis. "It isn't an ocean. [The water] is a very low percentage [of the rock], probably less than 0.1 percent." Given the region's size, however, that's enough to add up to a vast amount of water."

If you want archeological evidence of the flood, all you have to do is look at the dating of sites such as the step pyramid at Saqqara, they are said to date to 2750 BC. If you add that to the time that I wrote this book, 2009, you get 4759. The oldest thing living on earth today is an ancient bristlecone pine; it is estimated to be around 4767 years old. They only live in arid mountain regions in six western states of America and its date is almost the exact year as the pyramid. Gilgamesh built his city after a great flood around 2700 B.C. added to 2009 you get 4709. The starting point of the Mayan calendar is 3114 B.C. + 2009 = 5123. Not to mention the year 2009 will be 5769 in Hebrew and Abraham is dated to be born 6000 years ago, just after the time of the flood in the bible.

Other evidence supporting the occurrence of this flood can be found in places like Tiahuanaco. Tiahuanaco is located over 2 miles above sea level in the Bolivian Andes. It was built by an unknown group of people said to predate the Incas. We can verify this as being before the flood because it was located by a lake known as Lake Titicaca; Lake Titicaca meant "stone of the jaguar". It was given this name because when it was seen from the air, it had the shape of a jaguar getting ready to pounce. This was the only time in the ancient world that it is recorded that we were able to fly.

In this city, on top of the Kalassaya mound, was built the gateway of the sun. When it was unearthed, it was broken into two pieces. This gateway was carved from a single block of Andesite granite weighing approximately ten tons. Carved into the top of the archway is the figure of "Viracocha". On the head of "Viracocha" was carved the rays of the sun as his crown (crown of thorns) and on his face were carved tears running down his check. Around him are depicted 48 winged effigies, 32 with human faces, and 16 with condor heads. These effigies are the same types that were unearthed in Iraq, later translated to mean flight. Amongst these were found references to groups of men called the suncasapa, or "bearded ones", described as angelic warriors.

The Aymara Indians say that he was their savior; they say that he rose from Lake Titicaca to save them from the time of darkness. There story is the same as the rest of the people around the world for this time period. The people had displeased the gods and they destroyed the earth by flood. Viracocha is said to have disappeared by means of walking across the pacific ocean near Manta Ecuador, he is to reappear in times of trouble, (he is to reappear during the cross of the savior).

Most of the new construction of this city was found unfinished, like something had happened very fast. The ruins were found under 6 feet of earth, deeply buried in sediment that was saturated with marine life. This is believed by modern scholars to have only been possible at a time when water had quickly covered the land. Sadly, whatever they were trying to tell us is lost to mankind because the catholic missionaries destroyed much of the ruins and used them to build the local Catholic Church. If you are in doubt of what I am saying, you must take into consideration their quick appearance over and over, destroying and burning the remains of sites like these. By doing this, it would prevent you and your family from ever learning the things that I am trying to tell you.

Not to mention, the Hopi seem to be aware of these evil people because they claim that during the third world, the destruction happened so quickly, (verifying the story of Tiahuanaco) and was so intense, that there was a danger that the chosen people could have become corrupted before they could be led to the Ant kivas. They have two stories for the time of the flood. One says that Sotuknang told spider woman not to wait, but instead immediately create a way for the chosen people to escape. Spider woman then cut down large hollow reeds and sealed the people in with white cornmeal dough that they could eat.

As soon as they were sealed in, waves higher than mountains rolled in upon the land, continents broke apart and sank beneath the waves. It is said that great rains fell and added with the waves annihilating the third world by water. The other version of their story states that some of them hid underground; they say that these people emerged from a new crack in the earth that in my time was called the Grand Canyon. They called it the Sipapu, the "place of emergence".

Almost all native tribes that lived in the time that I wrote this book claim that the Grand Canyon was created as a result of the destruction that caused the great flood. They claim that it drowned the previous world for forgetting the story of creation and turning their minds away from natural things and toward metal and wheels. Things they could use to conquer and enslave their fellow man.

Interestingly enough, the sacred metal of this third world was copper. According to an article published on April 5, 1909 in the Phoenix Gazette, entitled "explorations in Grand Canyon: Mysteries of Immense rich cavern brought to light", two explorers, one by the name of G.E. Kinkaid, and the other Prof. S. A. Jordan, both from the Smithsonian institute, found an entrance in the Grand Canyon. The entrance was 42 miles up the river from the El Tovar Crystal canyon, approximately 2000 feet above the river bed on the east wall.

This entrance was said to be inaccessible from the top or bottom of the canyon without special equipment. The main passageway is around 12 feet wide, with a few feet of steps heading downward to the location of what is thought to be the level of the water in the time that it was occupied. More than a hundred feet from the entrance is the cross-hall, which is several hundred feet long. In the corner of this cross-hall, there were found a large number of tools, all of which were made of copper hardened to such strength it is said to be unmatched in my time.

In the opposite side of the cross-hall was a large idol or shrine that somewhat resembles Buddha or Brahma. Surrounding this idol were smaller images, some perfect in form, and others crooked necked and distorted. They were all carved out of a hard rock that was said to resemble marble. Further inside, the passages branch off to the right and left, and although not fully explored, they claim that some reach lengths that are believed to be over one mile. On both sides of some of these were rooms measuring in sizes up to 30 by 40 feet square.

These rooms are said to have oval shaped doors with walls around three feet six inches in thickness, in the rooms were vases, and cups of copper and gold. Also found were cats' eyes, yellow stones, all over the floor, each one engraved with the head of the Malay type. Over all of the doorways and tables of stone were mysterious hieroglyphs, of these there were only two pictorial writings of animals, one was prehistoric. Other passageways led to granaries which resembled the types found in oriental Temples.

In one of the largest chambers were several mummies, each one occupying a separate shelf type platform. At the head of each of these was a small bench; on top were copper cups and pieces of broken swords. All of the mummies were male and wrapped in a dark fabric, some were even covered in clay, no females or children were found. There were no bones of any type of animals, skins, no clothing or bedding. It is estimated that at one time, at least 50,000 people could have lived comfortably inside of this cavern. The religion that they were practicing was said to resemble the ancient people of Tibet.

According to the legend of the people of India, there is a race of people that live(d?) underground in the cities known as Patala and Bhogavati. They are known as the Nagas and are said to be a very advanced race with highly developed technology. It is said that the entrance to Bhogavati is somewhere in the Himalayas, the direction from which the Aryans came, and the entrance to Patala could be reached by going through the well of Sheshna in Benares, India. It is said that this entrance has 40 steps which stop at a closed stone door covered with cobra reliefs. The legends of Tibet say that the Patala tunnel system reaches not only throughout the Asian continent, but far beyond. It is my beliefs that because of the fact that the Hopi word for moon is the Tibetan word for sun, these tunnels could possibly even reach as far as the land of the Hopi, almost on the other side of the world. They may have even used a path formed by the waters of the underground ocean.

Manly P. Hall, 33rd degree mason, once stated "The explorers who opened the new world operated from a master plan and were agents of a re-discovery, rather then discoverers. Time will reveal that the continent now known as America was actually discovered and, to a considerable degree, explored more than a thousand years before the beginning of the Christian era. The true story was in the keeping of the Mystery Schools, and passed from them to the Secret Societies of the medieval world. The esoteric orders of Europe, Asia, and the Near East were in at least irregular communication with the priesthoods of the more advanced Amerindian nations. Plans for the development of the western hemisphere were formulated in Alexandria, Mecca, Delhi, and Lhasa (in Tibet) long before most European statesmen were aware of the great utopian program."

If you want to find the truth, you will have to let go of what they have taught you. These people are keeping from the world the information that led it to become as you see it today. They convinced almost everyone living in the time that I wrote this that they had no ideal about our past, it was all a lie. They did things like purposely try and teach everyone in their schools that Christopher Columbus discovered America. They thought of the people as ignorant, and they were. Most of them never even began to question what they were told until artifacts started to surface that suggested different.

For example, in 1957, a small boy found a coin in a field near Phenix City, Alabama. After some research, it was determined that the coin was made in Syracuse, on the island of Sicily, around 490 BC. Syracuse was once described by Cicero as "the greatest Greek city and the most beautiful of them all", it later became part of what is known as the Roman Republic.

In another incident in 1976, in a town known as Heavener, Oklahoma, a coin bearing the profile of the emperor Nero was found and identified as a bronze tetradrachm. After some study, it was determined that it was originally struck in Antioch, Syria, in 63 AD, Antioch, Syria was considered a cradle of gentile Christianity. Not to mention, in Texas, at the bottom of an Indian mound at

108

Round Rock, there were found Roman coins that dated to approximately 800 AD.

It is interesting to note that the present Indian tribes found in Arizona are direct descendants of the Asian people. They were thought of by most scholars to have been the slaves of the people that once inhabited the caves around the area of the Grand Canyon, they were not. They were the last of the people to have been given the knowledge of the gods. It is also interesting to note that even though they claim that the Anasazi are the descendents of the Hopi, to them, Anasazi means "enemy of my ancestors".

Chapter 6

The New Creator

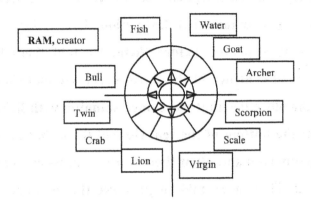

According to the Hopi, their last world was pushed underneath the water, exactly matching the story of Atlantis, the Mahabharata, and countless other stories around the world for this time. They say that the new world is the new backbone of the earth. The name given to this fourth world that Taiowa created was Tuwaqachi, Tuwaqachi means "world complete", it is the last world of this ancient cycle of the zodiac, it is the beginning of the end of the cycle of time.

The Hopi say that after the waters started to reseed, the chosen people found their reeds on the top of a mountain in which there was no land in sight. They sent birds into the air in search of land but found none. After this, the chosen people constructed rafts and let the forces of the earth guide them. It is said that they passed many islands as they crossed the pacific to the deserts southwest, finally reaching their intended destination. There, they say that Sotuknang appeared before them. He told them he washed away all evidence of the third world. He told them that all of the old cities that were once shinning with lights were now at the bottom of the sea. He told them that all of the flying patuwvota and all of their worldly treasures were there as well. They were told to preserve the memory of their emergence into this fourth world so that when these places rise again, it will prove the words that they speak.

It is at this time that the Hopi refer to Masaw. They say he was appointed as caretaker over the land of the new world. They say that they were warned to go out and claim the land under the permission of Masaw. They were told to divide into groups and begin their migrations to their chosen lands. "may we meet again" they all called back to each other.

They say when Masaw gave the people the chosen directions to their place in this new world. He wrote the instructions on tablets so that they would never forget. The directions written on them led them to settle in there new location by spreading out in the shape of a swastika. They say that each of the four tribes were supposed to follow their stars toward the four cardinal directions and when they reached the place where the land met the sea, they were to turn right on this path for a certain distance and then right again in a spiral pattern until they reached their destination. Everywhere they went, they were to carve on the rocks their signatures and pictographs to identify them, their migrations, and their history. The Hopi claim that they are still in possession of these stone tablets and describe them as being made of a stone that is not found in America. They are said to resemble ivory and have written on them hieroglyphs similar to those found in Egyptian temples.

Another reason why we know that these people were Asian is because these same directions were given to the sons of Japheth, they were told to follow this same pattern from their place of emergence. Japheth was the son of Noah and their symbol was the swastika. The Hopi claim that they were to repeat this migrations process for the purpose of purification. They say that these ceremonies were performed for the purpose of weeding out all of the evil people that may have lived through the destruction of the previous Third World. They claim that man was not supposed to succumb to the comfort and luxury that could be given to him by his surroundings because he would lose the need to rely upon the Creator.

In 1995 Dr. John Coleman Darnell, a Yale Egyptologist along with his wife, Dr. Deborah Carnell, also an Egyptologist, set out to survey ancient trade routes west of the Nile in Gebel Tjauti. There they discovered carved in the limestone of a desert cliff, a 5,250-year-old tableau, measuring 18 by 20 inches. "We do feel that this is the earliest known historical document," John Darnell stated in an interview. "It may not be exactly 100 percent writing, only proto-hieroglyphs, but the tableau really is able to impart the who, what, where of an event."

Renee Friedman, an Egyptologist at the British Museum in London, who has examined the tableau, said, "It is a historical document, there's no question about it." On it is a carving of what is said to be the falcon god Horus, the falcon is one of the symbols of the god Zeus. Next to it, there is a figure holding a staff and a long-necked bird with a serpent in its beak. This story is the same one that is told in all of the pyramids; it is the representation of the defeat of Ea's people.

This tableau depicts a bound prisoner with long hair being held by a rope which is connected to a bearded man with close cropped hair. He is holding a weapon that is known as a mace, and it looks as if he is leading a fallen

114

ruler to his execution. Behind the prisoner is a carving of a bull's head on a staff,. It was the descendants of the cult of Sin who were referred to as the lord of the cowherders, they were the ones whom used this symbolism. They did so to not only represent Zeus, who wore a crown with two horns on his head, but to represent the conquering of the age of the bull as well.

They were the keepers of the tablet of destiny and the knowledge of the zodiac. This knowledge was passed down to the tribe of Sin because he was the first born son of Enlil/Zeus. It was because of his knowledge that this tribe was able to conquer the age of the bull. This gave Sin the titles, "lord of the cowherders" and "Lord of the calendar". He was known as the one "who determines the destinies of distant days and whose plans no god knows". One of the first places that the descendants of Zeus show up after the flood is Iraq.

Iraq is not only where the oldest stories of the bible come from, but the cult of Sin hailed from Ur in Iraq by way of Harran. According to Genesis, Abraham hailed from Ur in Iraq by way of Harran. It is in Sumeria, in Iraq, where the oldest Zodiac calendar was found. The knowledge of this zodiac was considered by these people to be the most important knowledge known to the gods, and because of the ignorance of the followers of Zeus, no mixed

115

breed race would ever have this knowledge again until I was able to decipher the messages left by Ea's people almost 4,000 years later.

Now although it is most commonly believed that the descendants of Poseidon lived on the island of Atlantis, located in the Atlantic Ocean, due to the description left by Plato, they did not, they lived on the island of Mu. There are many many stories of the lost island of Mu, sometimes referred to as Lemuria. According to the traditions of many Pacific islands, Mu was an ancient tropical paradise located somewhere in the Pacific. It is said to have sunk along with all of its beautiful inhabitants, thousands of years ago.

The descendants of Ea, the Asians, can be found on every shore surrounding the ocean of the pacific. They occupied the territories all the way to the pyramids of Egypt, the location where the three allotted territories of the three races came together; it was the place where the three kings made their first pact. This can easily be verified by taking a globe and applying the concept of Pangaea. The word Pangaea was fist given by the German meteorologist and geologist, Alfred Wegener to describe how the continents once fit together.

It states that Millions of years ago, the earth was smaller; as it has expanded, it has broken apart. The places that break apart, become lower than sea level, and fill with

116

water. This is how the Hopi claim the Grand Canyon was formed in the forth world. If you equally shrink back down the globe from all directions, at the point where all of the continents meet, eliminating the water, the only place that is left, is a patch of islands in the Pacific Ocean. Plato stated, "there are remaining only the bones of the wasted body, as they may be called, as in the case of small islands, all the richer and softer parts of the soil having fallen away." The shores that remain are the shores that are the most concentrated with the remnants of the people of the serpent, the Asians. In fact, the center of the Pacific Ocean is one of the only bodies of water in the world in which you can leave in four different directions, form a perfect swastika, and be in the location of almost all of the pyramids on earth. That is why the Asians were the first ones to reach the New World, (America) after the flood.

We also know they reached America first after the flood because of evidence in Structures such as California's East Bay Walls. In 1904, Dr. John Fryer, a professor of Oriental languages at U.C. Berkeley, publicly stated: "This is undoubtedly the work of Mongolians... the Chinese would naturally wall themselves in, as they do in all of their towns in China." Later, underwater expeditions off the coast of California yielded stone anchors and line weights made in the style of the ancient Chinese. And if you want to compare

the dating of the coins found to the ones of the Romans. Not far away in British Columbia, in the summer of 1882, a miner found 30 Chinese coins, 25 feet below the surface. After they were examined, it was determined that the coins were invented by the Emperor Huungt, around 2637 BC.

These discoveries give weight to claims of a lost civilization discovered off the southern shore of Okinawa, Japan, under 20 to 100 feet of water. This city is spread out over 311 miles across the ocean floor, from the waters of Okinawa, to the small island of Yonaguni, and dates to around 8,000 BC. These cities are said to have long paved streets, with staircases leading to archways built out of enormous blocks that are perfectly cut and fitted together in a style of architecture that very much resembles that found in Tiahuanaco, high in the Andes Mountains of Peru.

In an article entitled "Divers Find World's Oldest Building" written by Trushar Barot, it stated, "A structure thought to be the world's oldest building, nearly twice the age of the great pyramids of Egypt, has been discovered. The rectangular stone ziggurat under the sea off the coast of Japan could be the first evidence of a previously unknown Stone Age civilization, say archeologists. The monument is 600ft wide and 90ft high and has been dated to at least 8000BC."

The first scientist to investigate the site was Professor Masaki Kimura, a geologist at Ryukyu University in Okinawa. In a statement to the public he said "The object has not been manufactured by nature. If that had been the case, one would expect debris from erosion to have collected around the site, but there are no rock fragments there," He stated that "The structure could be an ancient religious shrine, possibly celebrating an ancient deity resembling the god Nirai-Kanai, whom locals say gave happiness to the people of Okinawa from beyond the sea. This could be evidence of a new culture as there are no records of a people intelligent enough to have built such a monument 10,000 years ago," he goes on saying, "This could only have been done by a people with a high degree of technology, probably coming from the Asian continent, where the oldest civilizations originate. There would have to have been some sort of machinery involved to have created such a huge structure."

In an article written by Frank Joseph, the editor in chief of Ancient American magazine, he stated "Nothing about it has been mentioned in any of the nation's other archaeology publications, not even in any of our daily newspapers. One would imagine that such a mind-boggling find would be the most exciting piece of news an archaeologist could possibly hope to learn. Even so, outside

119

of the "Ancient American" and CNN's single report, the pall of silence covering all the facts about Okinawa's structures screens them from view more effectively then their location at the bottom of the sea. Why? How can this appalling neglect persist in the face of a discovery of such unparalleled magnitude? At the risk of accusations of paranoia, one might conclude that a real conspiracy of managed information dominates America's well-springs of public knowledge."

An archeologist at University College London, by the name of Jim Mower, stated "If it is confirmed that the site is as old as 10,000 years and is man-made, then this is going to change an awful lot of the previous thinking on Southeast Asian history. It would put the people who made the monument on a par with the ancient civilization of Mesopotamia and the Indus Valley." This is not a coincidence; the first signs of civilization in Japan are found in the Neolithic period around 11,000 years ago, the exact date of the ending of the age of the destroyer. These are all civilizations that were first started by Ea/Poseidon in the beginning of the age of the creator.

Some of the temples that the descendants later built, like the great pyramids of Giza, still have the depictions of the new race of people that was talked about in the bible painted on the walls. In these pyramids you can plainly see depicted a race of people that is half African, and half Asian, their eyes are a dead give away. It was on these same walls that they had added the "key of life", the ankh, to give the people the knowledge of the gods.

They depicted the ankh to be represented on top of the lion and the Virgin of the Zodiac, as represented by the original design of the Sphinx, with the head of a virgin, and the body of a lion. Robert Bauval stated in "The Age of the Sphinx", "there was no inscriptions - not a single one - either carved on a wall or a stela or written on the throngs of papyri" that associates the Sphinx with this time period", the time in which the hieroglyphs were placed in the pyramids. The purpose of the new depictions in these pyramids was to show the people of the future the time of the next global catastrophe. With this knowledge, they would know that in order to live through it, they would have to start preparing in the age of the savior, just like the original designers of the Sphinx did for the coming of the younger Dryas.

The top of the ankh is what was known in my time as the omega symbol. It was put there to represent the ending of the age of Pisces, the beginning of the Age of Aquarius. One of the oldest depictions of this Omega symbol was found with Lilith. She was depicted as standing on the back of a lion with a water pitcher in one hand, and the ring of Shem in the other. The ring of shem was the original depiction of the omega symbol and its depiction in her hand represented her knowledge of the gods. Among some of the other hieroglyphs were "flying boats" and flying disks that "shined of many colors."

The people that occupied the land of Egypt in the time in which I lived had no idea what these symbols meant. Those pyramids were part of the first territories that the cult of Zeus had taken control of after the flood. The bible written by the cult of Zeus to represent this age, stole the stories of Ea's people and made them their own. They made the people think that the descendants of the serpent were evil, so the people would only trust them. They could not tell them the truth; they could not tell them that Ea/Poseidon and his descendants were the only ones who were trying to help them.

In fact, in the Epic of Gilgamesh, and the story of Utnapishtim, it is more than likely that he was living on one of the islands located in the Pacific. Stories like the birth of Moses were taken from Sargon, known as Sargon the great, or the true king. He was the founder of the dynasty of Akkad, which the king list claims he built. He was born in secret and set in a basket with the lid sealed, then cast into a river. He captured Uruk which Gilgamesh had built, Gilgamesh was half man and half god, forbidden by Zeus, then dismantled its walls. The people there fled and joined forces with Lugal-Zage-Si, and after he was defeated, Sargon took him to the gates of Enlil/Zeus in a dog collar. A story that is very similar to the one that was depicted on the tableau that was found, by Dr. John Coleman Darnell and his wife, Dr. Deborah Carnell, west of the Nile in Gebel Tjauti.

The only thing that the followers of Zeus ever had to do to verify the fact that the bible they were reading was misleading, was read the Tempest Stele. It was erected by Ahmose around 1550 BC, and was found in the 3rd pylon in the Temple of Karnack at Thebes. It was restored as much as possible, translated, then published by Claude Vandersleyen in 1967, he later added to it pieces found during the cleaning of the foundation. This date was not only the time that is said to be the Exodus of the Bible, but it was also the only disaster that the occupants felt worthy of recording. These records indicate that during a war with the Hyksos, which comes from the Egyptian Hikau Khausut, meaning rulers of foreign countries, there was a great storm.

Their headquarters was the island of Crete, which was at the time of this storm, destroyed by the eruption of Thera, also known as the Santorini eruption. Before the eruption, they had ruled the lower and middle Egypt for

108 years after building atop a middle city that was either capture by them or covered by the flood. The same story can be found in the Ipuwer papyrus, and the El-Arish which calls them "invaders", and refers to them as the "evil ones".

To get rid of these evil invaders, the tempest stele describes the things demanded by the tribe of Zeus. Once given, these things were not only used to build a movable temple, but they were also used to build the ark that housed the newly stolen tablet of destiny which had been handed down to the descendants of Poseidon. The Tempest Stele states that his majesty provided "them with silver, with gold, with copper, with cloth, with all the products they desired." They had no ideal that the sacred temple had been broken into. It is at this time that the descendants of the cult of Sin, are said to posses the knowledge that no god knows. The tempest stele states: "It was then that his majesty was informed that the funerary concessions had been invaded...that the sepulchral chambers had been damaged, that the structures of funerary enclosures had been undermined."

In the time that I lived, on the other side of the world, in the region known as North America, you could not go five minutes without seeing the star of Athena on TV. This star and eagle of Zeus actually represented the country that I lived, the new Atlantis. Fifty-two of the 55 founders of the Constitution of this country were members of the established orthodox churches; they were members of the cult of Zeus.

In this land known as America, the most famous people were actually called stars. If you were able to achieve their status, you would be represented with the symbol of Athena. This symbol not only represented our military, but it also represented the states in our country. It was placed on the chests and the cars of the people that enforced the laws, and the more people you killed for this country in battle, the more stars of Athens you could receive, you could actually get up to five. In fact, I tried to count how many time I either heard, or located, this star on TV, in an 8 hour period, and I lost track at 164.

To me, the strangest thing of all was that the people of my time did not even find this odd, I cannot remember one time in my life that anybody ever even mentioned this. It was almost like they were completely mindless, like they had been brainwashed to only see what the cult of Zeus wanted them too. The sad thing was, I honestly could not rule this out as fact, they controlled the schools, the television programs, and the news papers, which referred to God (Zeus) and how great he was, equally to the times you would see his daughters' symbol.

Not far from where I lived, in the Mexican valley, Ea's people had built the Aztec Pyramids. Like all of the rest of the pyramids that they had built, they were positioned like giant celestial calendars. The most well known of these Aztec pyramids was the Templo Mayor, this pyramid was the main temple and capital of Tenochititlan, it was designed as a step pyramid and stood 197 feet above the city.

In this territory, Ea/Poseidon was referred to as Quetzalcoatl, and the temples were dedicated to him because he had seeded their race. He was depicted at the ends of some of the stairs as a Serpent, the keeper of time. Zeus was represented with a Stone eagle that was placed on the temples at Tepoztlan, the Temple of the Feathered Serpent in Xochicalco, the round temple of Cempoala, and the temple of Ehecatl in Calixtlahuaca. In their language Zeus was called Huitzilopochtli-Tonatiuh. Huitzilopochtli was described in the temples as the god of war and the sun. Inside these temples told the story of how Zeus had sacrificed 84,000 of Ea's people.

The stories that escaped the wrath of this cult matched the rest that can be found around the world. They say Quetzalcoatl/Ea descended from a "hole in the sky" when he came to Mexico. He is described as descending in a winged ship in which he sailed, the same winged ships that

126

were found depicted in Egypt. They say he instructed the Central American Indians in the sciences of agriculture, astronomy, architecture, and gave them a code of ethics. He was called Viracocha by the Incas and Kukulkan by the Mayans.

The Mayans and Aztecs describe this feathered serpent god as being white, with large eyes and having a flowing beard. He wore a long white robe reaching to his feet and referred to himself as the God of Peace. He was depicted as descending from the sky with a rope ladder to bring civilization to earth. It should have never been thought of as odd at all when in 1914, an archaeologist by the name of M.A. Gonzales, while excavating some Mayan ruins in the city of Acajutla, Mexico, discovered what appeared to be two Egyptian statuettes depicting Osiris and Isis.

On June 15, 1952, Alfred Ruz and his excavation crew located a Mayan tomb that had been hidden away for over twelve centuries. On the sarcophagus was what appeared to be a machine from a culture supposedly without wheels? It showed a well shaved man that was wearing clothing that looked a lot like a close-fitting space-suit. The man was depicted as half way lying on a wrapping seat that held his lower back and thighs. The back of his neck was reclined on a head-rest and his hands appeared to be operating various levers, controls, and dials. The man is incased in this machine that appears to have some type of propulsion system that is driving him forward. It is believed by many to be the depiction of someone either in flight, or a vehicle designed to navigate the miles of tunnels found under the earth, in either case, the site is referred to as the "Tomb of the Astronaut".

Located in what is now the desert region of Iran, there exists a series of caves. On the walls inside of some of these caves, archaeologists have discovered prehistoric paintings that depict "circles of fire" in the sky. Not far from those same caves is the city of Sumer. The story associated with the birth of this city says that a flying ship landed on the shores of the Persian Gulf and the occupant appeared as a large fish with a human face in its mouth. The dwellers of Mesopotamia knew him as Oannes, and claim he taught them how to build cities, compile laws, plant wheat, write down thoughts, count with numbers and observe the stars.

The god that was depicted to represent the age of the flood was known as Hathor. She was known as the eye of Amen Ra, the sun god, the creator of the forth world. It was Amen Ra who gave forth light so that the plants could grow to nourish the people of this world. She was the representation of the ancient knowledge of the Milky Way.

She was known as "the milk that flowed from the udders of a heavenly cow". An alternate name for her was Mehturt, Mehturt means "great flood". She was depicted as a cow deity to represent the age of the bull, the age of the destroyer.

60 kilometers north of Luxor, on the west bank of the Nile River, exists a temple that is dedicated to Hathor, it is known as the temple of Dendera. This temple is one of the oldest and best preserved temples in Egypt. Among the depictions were found flying disks and what was known as the Dendera zodiac. This zodiac contained many of the same symbols as the zodiac that is referred to in this book. In 1820, a master mason removed the circular zodiac with saws, jacks, and scissors constructed special for the job.

Depicted on the wall of one of the lower chambers of the temple of Hathor was what appeared to be a light bulb, the element was made up of a glowing snake. In 1936, a few hundred kilometers east of Egypt, in Iraq, strange pots were found. Some of them contained watertight copper cylinders, glued into the opening with asphalt. In the middle of these cylinders were iron rods, held in place with asphalt as well. The design matched closely to the way the batteries were designed in my time. Iraq was one the trading posts of India, the people of the Gods.

In the ancient Indian text Agasthya Samhita, it describes how to make these electrical batteries, it states, "Place a well-cleaned copper plate in an earthenware vessel. Cover it first by copper sulfate and then moist sawdust. After that put a mercury-amalgamated-zinc sheet on top of an energy known by the twin name of Mitra-Varuna. Water will be split by this current into Pranavayu and Udanavayu." According to the text, a chain of one hundred jars will give a very active and effective force. Note that the word varuna is what we called in my time an anode, Pranavayu means oxygen, udanavayu means hydrogen and mitra is a cathode.

Chapter 7

The New Creator Part Two

The people that were assigned to kill off the descendants of Ea and build the new cities of this new world were referred to in my time as Masons. They were the descendants of the caretaker of the new world in which the Native Americans referred to as Masaw. These people were the messengers/angels of the descendents of the god Zeus. 33rd degree Mason, Foster bailey once stated: "Masonry is the descendant of, or is founded upon, a divinely imparted religion which long antedates the prime date of creation as given in our bible. It is all that remains to us of the first world religion which flourished in an antiquity so old that it is impossible to affix a date. It was the first unified religion... To this, such symbols as the pyramids, both in Egypt and South America, bear witness... The ancient mysteries were temporary custodians of the ancient truth and closely allied to the Masonic work of today... The relation of the mysteries to masonry has oft been recognized, and the golden thread of living continually can be traced through them to modern masonry. The mysteries... Are all parts of that ancient thread which has its origin in that primeval religion which terminates today in masonry."

When speaking of the knowledge that was taught to these masons, 33rd degree mason Manly Hall stated, "the age of the Masonic school is not to be calculated by hundreds or even thousands of years, for it never had any origin in the worlds of form. It is a shadow of the great Atlantean mystery school, which stood with all it's splendor in the ancient city of the golden gates, where now the turbulent Atlantic rolls in unbroken sweep". In the bible, this was the description of Heaven, the "city of the golden gates".

These people run a secret organization that controls every thought, vision, or invention, that is implanted into the minds of the people of this fourth world. Marie Bauer Hall once stated "Though the whole extent and origin of the plan was known only to an initiate few, members of the outer order were subjected to a selective system by which they could attain to numerous degrees and proportionately received deeper insight into the work. This in turn spurred them to greater effort and endeavor to in their various occupations and stations in life, and made them useful instruments."

The people who are at the bottom of this pyramid scheme never know the true reason for the things that they do. 33rd degree mason, Adam Weishaupt, spoke of this stating, "The great strength of our order lies in its concealment. Let it never appear in any place in its own name, but always covered by another name, and another occupation. None is fitter than the three lower degrees of the Free Masonry, the public is accustomed to it, expect little from it, and therefore takes little notice of it. Next to this, the form of a learned or literary society is best suited to our purpose, and had Free Masonry not existed, this cover would have been employed, and it may be much more than the cover, it may be a powerful engine in our hands. By establishing reading societies, and subscription libraries, but if we may turn the public mind which way we will. In like manner we must try to obtain an influence in all offices which have any effect, either in forming, or in managing, or even in directing the mind of man."

33rd degree mason, General Albert Pike spoke of these lower degrees stating, "The Blue Degrees are but the outer court or portico of the Temple. Part of the symbols are displayed there to the Initiate, but he is intentionally misled by false interpretations. It is not intended that he shall understand them; but it is intended that he shall imagine he understands them. Their true explanation is reserved for the Adepts, the Princes of Masonry."

The Apprentice Mason Oath, 1st Degree states, "To all of which I do most solemnly and sincerely promise and swear, without the least equivocation, mental reservation, or evasion of mind in me whatever; binding myself under no less penalty than to have my throat cut across, my tongue torn out by the roots, and my body buried in the rough sands of the sea at low water-mark, where the tide ebbs and flows twice in twenty-four hours; so help me God, and keep me steadfast in the due performance of the same."

The Fellow Craft Mason Oath, 2nd Degree states, "Binding myself under no less penalty than to have my left breast torn open and my heart and vitals taken from thence and thrown over my left shoulder and carried into the valley of Jehosaphat, there to become a prey to the wild beasts of the field, and vulture of the air, if ever I should prove willfully guilty of violating any part of this my solemn oath or obligation of a Fellow Craft Mason; so help me God, and keep me steadfast in the due performance of the same."

And the Master Mason Blood Oath, 3rd Degree states, "Binding myself under no less penalty than to have my body severed in two in the midst, and divided to the north and south, my bowels burnt to ashes in the center, and the ashes scattered before the four winds of heaven, that there might not the least track or trace of remembrance remain among men or Masons, of so vile and perjured a wretch as I should be, were I ever to prove willfully guilty of violating any part of this my solemn oath or obligation of a Master Mason. So help me God, and keep me steadfast in the performance of the same."

It is because of the fact that these people controlled everything in the beginning of the building of the fourth world that they were able to guide the people in whatever direction they wanted. Stephen Knight stated, "The more masons there are in any area or profession the more important it is to be a Mason if one is not to risk losing out, as a non-member of the club, in one's business, one's profession and ones preferment. In many fields nowadays the disadvantage of being left out of the club are perceived as being too serious for a great many people to contemplate, what ever they may feel personally about the morality of joining a secrets society, or about the misty tenets of speculative Freemasonry."

After searching through all of their little clues, and combining all of their ancient symbols. The bottom line is, without a doubt, the cult of Zeus was killing and stealing the territories that were allotted to the people of Poseidon in the beginning of the third world. They first took from these descendants the great pyramids of Egypt, where they stole the tablet of destiny and housed it in the ark. The bible states in Joshua that they then made their way across the Jordan River. In the ancient Indian texts speaking of the same time it picks up with them burning the lands of Afghanistan as they moved into the territories of India.

In the bible, Exodus 13:21-22 it states "The Lord was going before them in a pillar of cloud by day to lead them on the way, and in a pillar of fire by night to give them light, that they might travel by day and by night. He did not take away the pillar of cloud by day, nor the pillar of fire by night, from before the people". The followers of this cult in my time thought that this was some great thing that this god had done. If they would have just taken the time to study the history of the past, they would have found that this was no more than a slaughter of innocent men, women, and babies that were left for dead in a pile of burning flesh as they stole their land and possessions.

According to the Indian texts, when these people finally reached the land of India, they not only destroyed all of the written records of their past, but they killed off all but one race that lived there. They then assigned to them a new language, Sanskrit. In my time, this writing was found throughout the north of the sub continent across Pakistan, India, and Bangladesh. It was the root of the languages spoken by nearly a billion people.

A Welch judge named William Jones, who was the founder of the Asiatic society, gave a lecture on February 2, 1786, stating the similarities between Sanskrit, Latin, Greek, English and Welsh. He noticed that the word father was vater in German, in Latin pater, and pitar in Sanskrit. He also noticed that the word for mother was mater in Latin, meter in Greek, and matar in Sanskrit. The word for horse in Sanskrit was aszwa, thousands of miles away in Lithuania it was asva, almost exactly the same. Jones stated "no philologer could examine them all three, without believing them to have sprung from some common source." These people can be traced to being responsible for starting no less than modern English, German, French, Latin, Greek, Persian, and Sanskrit.

Their invasion of the people of India plummeted the civilization into 2500 years of almost complete darkness. This time period, was reported as lasting from 1500 BC to 1000 AD, it was known as the Vedic Dark Ages. It is during this time that these people not only destroyed the irrigation systems, but they used their knowledge of roots to poison their water. This not only ended the production of agriculture in the region, but it completely wiped out all existence of Ea's people from the surrounding areas.

This was the first recorded instance of ecological warfare in the new world. The only people that were allowed to live were the people that agreed to be part of the slave race of Zeus; they were given the land of India for their cooperation. The Vedic religion actually states that this Aryan race is superior to all other races and is hence justified in massacring, looting and ruling over all other people.

Their belief in this system was well documented in their bible, in verses such as Exodus 21:20-21 it states "When a man strikes his male or female slave with a rod so hard that the slave dies under his hand, he shall be punished. If, however, the slave survives for a day or two, he is not to be punished, since the slave is his own property." After the Aryan invasion, the existence of the building of the ziggurat pyramids stopped.

When the cities of India were built again, it was done so by the angelic warrior/masons as ordered by the cult of Zeus while they continued on their extermination of all traces of the territories that were left. The beginning of this slaughter that took place at the start of the age of the ram was recorded in the bible when Moses came down from the mountain after receiving the laws for the new age. It is at this time that these slaves were still worshipping a golden (sun) calf, the sacred cow India, the age of Taurus.

In the bible Moses commands a great slaughter to destroy the knowledge of the old age of the bull and bring in the new age of Aries, the Ram. Exodus 32:27 "get your swords and go back and forth from one end of the camp to the other and kill even your brothers, friends, and neighbors." Exodus 32:35 "and the lord sent a great plague upon the people because they had worshipped Aaron's calf." This started the blowing of the ram's horn and the enslavement of Jericho around four thousand years ago. The Jews still did this in the time that I wrote this book, they were left behind, just like the slaves of India had been in the previous age.

They had the same feature as the people of India, but their skin color was a little lighter. They were assigned a new god as the creator, and he was referred to by them as Jehovah. This new race was promised a section of land for their help, just like what was promised to the slaves of India. If they did not help, they were to be killed. This land is referred to in the bible as the Promised Land.

2 Chronicles 15:12-13 "They entered into a covenant to seek the Lord, the God of their fathers, with all their heart and soul; and everyone who would not seek the Lord, the God of Israel, was to be put to death, whether small or great, whether man or woman." They made it law, punishable by death that there was to be no more temples built for the worship of Poseidon and his people. Exodus

22:19 "Whoever sacrifices to any god, except the Lord alone, shall be doomed."

Deuteronomy 13:13-19 "Suppose you hear in one of the towns the LORD your God is giving you that some worthless rabble among you have led their fellow citizens astray by encouraging them to worship foreign gods. In such cases, you must examine the facts carefully. If you find it is true and can prove that such a detestable act has occurred among you, you must attack that town and completely destroy all its inhabitants, as well as all the livestock. Then you must pile all the plunder in the middle of the street and burn it. Put the entire town to the torch as a burnt offering to the LORD your God. That town must remain a ruin forever; it may never be rebuilt. Keep none of the plunder that has been set apart for destruction. Then the LORD will turn from his fierce anger and be merciful to you. He will have compassion on you and make you a great nation, just as he solemnly promised your ancestors. "The LORD your God will be merciful only if you obey him and keep all the commands I am giving you today, doing what is pleasing to him."

Everyone except the descendants of the god Zeus, who had the knowledge to read the heavens, was to be killed, wiped of the face of the earth as well. Deuteronomy 17:2-5 "Suppose a man or woman among you, in one of

140

your towns that the LORD your God is giving you, has done evil in the sight of the LORD your God and has violated the covenant by serving other gods or by worshiping the sun, the moon, or any of the forces of heaven, which I have strictly forbidden. When you hear about it, investigate the matter thoroughly. If it is true that this detestable thing has been done in Israel, then that man or woman must be taken to the gates of the town and stoned to death."

Deuteronomy 13:7-12 "If your own full brother, or your son or daughter, or your beloved wife, or your intimate friend, entices you secretly to serve other gods, whom you and your fathers have not known, gods of any other nations, near at hand or far away, from one end of the earth to the other: do not yield to him or listen to him, nor look with pity upon him, to spare or shield him, but kill him. Your hand shall be the first raised to slay him; the rest of the people shall join in with you. You shall stone him to death, because he sought to lead you astray from the Lord, your God." It is during this age after being pushed into a corner that the descendant of Ea/Poseidon began to build what is referred to as "The Great Wall of China" in 656 BC. They also began to bury the rest of their pyramids under dirt to make them appear as natural hills.

In the time that I lived, most of the people had no ideal that many of the pyramids of China matched exactly to those found everywhere else in the world, they had no ideal that some of the pyramids that existed there were larger than the great pyramid of Egypt. Not only this, but they were built with the same concept in mind. They all had four sides and were built to the alignment of the stars. The ancient Chinese writing of that time is not only very similar to the writings found at the Mayan site, but they speak of their emperors descending from heaven in flying dragons.

In 1912, two travel agents by the name of Fred Meyer Schroder and Oscar Maman, for the first time ever, reported these pyramids to the western world, they stated "It was more eerie than if we had found them in the wilderness. Here they have been under the nose of the world, but unknown to the western countries... The big pyramid is about 1,000 feet high and roughly 1,500 feet at the base, which makes it twice as large as any pyramid in Egypt. The four faces of the structure are oriented with the compass points." The reporting of this was pushed aside to make way for the sinking of the Titanic. The Titanic was a large passenger ship owned by 33rd degree mason J.P. Morgan.

Later James Gaussman and his co-pilot stated after having technical difficulties which led them off course while flying During the second world war, "I banked to avoid a mountain and we came out over a level valley. Directly below was a gigantic white pyramid. It looked like something out of a fairy tale. It was encased in shimmering white. This could have been metal, or some sort of stone. It was pure white on all sides. The remarkable thing was the capstone, a huge piece of jewel-like material that could have been crystal. There was no way we could have landed, although we wanted to. We were struck by the immensity of the thing."

This led to the existence of these pyramids being reported again in 1947 in "The New York Times". Two days later in the "New York Sunday News", an article was published with a photo. Some sources say the photo was then confiscated and placed in the files of the US Military were it did not surface again until 45 years later. Whether the confiscation was true or not really doesn't matter because the fact was, the story was quickly replaced by a report of a UFO crashing in Roswell, New Mexico. The media was then flooded with stories of the building of the pyramids by Aliens (Asians). The reporting of this crash kept secret from the people of my country, for almost the rest of their lives, the fact that there are more pyramids in China than anywhere else in the world.

Here is a list of some of the pyramid coordinates (locations), I am listing only a few because there are more than a hundred.

(34°20'17"N108°34'11"E)

(34°21'47.16"N108°37'49.80"E)

(34°21'42.48"N108°38'24.3"E)

(34°22'29.64"N108°41'51.36"E)

(34°23'52"N108°42'43"E)

(34°14'09.00"N109°07'05.00"E)

(34°10'45.00"N109°01'41.00"E)

(34°22'52"N109°15'12"E)

This is a list of some of the religions that were started before the new age religion of Jesus Christ, the newest savior. Anyone who knew their purpose in the age of the creator was to be exterminated in order to insure that the people would never understand the story of creation. With no knowledge of the time before the flood, the people of my time gave these religions the best dates they could, sadly, they were completely in the dark to the system that they were put in place for, they claim.

Dionysus 500 BC., Quirinus 506 BC., Prometheus 547 BC., Wittoba 552 BC., Quexalcote 587 BC., Hindoo Sakia 600 BC., Alcestos 600 BC., Iao 622 BC., Bali 725 BC., Indra 725 BC., Hesus 834 BC. Tammuz (Greek Adonis)(see Ezekiel

144

8:8-16) 1160 BC., Mithra 1170 BC., Atys 1170 BC., Crite 1200 BC., Thulis 1700 BC., ...Eusebius of Caesarea (283-371) wrote, "The religion of Jesus Christ is neither new nor strange."

In Greek mythology, Prometheus is a Titan who is known for his intelligence. It is Prometheus who was known for stealing the secrets of Zeus and giving them to mortal men. He is attributed to stealing and giving no less than the arts of civilization, writing, mathematics, agriculture, medicine, science, and the saving of them from complete destruction due to the fact that Zeus had wanted to obliterate the entire human race. Zeus later punishes him for his crimes by having him bound to a rock while a great eagle ate at his liver. He was claimed by a number of ancient sources to have played a pivotal role in the early history of human kind.

At this point, it is interesting to note two different facts. One is the fact that in Genesis 16:2-3, it tells the story of Hagar, an Egyptian servant belonging to Sarah, who, being barren, gave Hagar to her husband Abraham "to be his wife", so that he might still have children. She gave birth to a son, whom she named Ishmael. Fourteen years after this, God allowed Sarah to give birth to Isaac. According to Genesis, God commanded Abraham to obey Sarah's wishes and expel Hagar and Ishmael into the wilderness. At first, Abraham was reluctant to send his son away, but God promised to make a great nation out of him. After Abraham agreed, this branch of the family tree became the Muslim religion.

The second fact is, it is more than likely that the territory of China was taken over by the descendants of Zeus. I mention this because around the year 0, the first emperor of China, Qin Shi Huang, ordered all of their history to be burned and copies stored. This blatant disregard for the feelings of the people and their past matched exactly to the deeds ordered by the descendants of Zeus. Anyone who tried to save their works were rounded up, given a mark like the one referred to in the bible, used for hard labor, and later slaughtered, or worked to death. Before Qin Shi Huang died, legend says he sent out spies in search of eternal life but they were stopped by giant fish, the symbol of Pisces, the symbol of the new religious order of Jesus.

146

Chapter 8

The New Age Savior

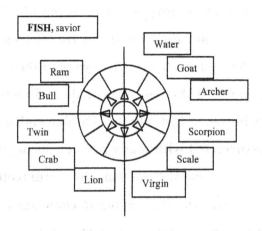

Around 2000 years ago, or the year 0, Jesus fed his followers with two fishes, the constellation of Pisces. It is in this age of the savior that the new god Jesus, "the savior", was born as the constellation of Pisces first appeared in the sky. He was then visited by wise men or shepherds guided by a star. The moment he was born his surroundings were splendidly illuminated. He was recognized, and adored by people who prostrated themselves before this heaven-born child. He was born at a time when his foster father was away from home, having come to the city to pay his tax or yearly tribute. He was born in a state most abject and humiliating. His earthly father was a carpenter. His father was warned by a heavenly voice because the reigning monarch sought his life. The monarch ordered the massacre in all his states of all the children of the male sex born during the night of his birth. One of the first miracles he performed when mature was the curing of a leper. He cast out demons and raised the dead. He selected disciples to spread his teachings. He was the second of the trinity.

He was called the lion of his tribe. He was without sin. He celebrated a last supper. He descended into hell only to be resurrected with many people viewing his ascent into heaven. He claimed "I am the resurrection". He forgave his enemies and he is going to come again on earth and appear among mortals as an armed warrior, riding a white horse. At his approach the sun and moon will be darkened, the earth tremble and the stars will fall from the firmament.

The fact is, the main reason why there are more than one hundred similarities between Jesus of Christianity and Krishna, is because they were both put in place by the same organization, the same organization that declared the slaughter of all of the people of the serpent race for the purpose of keeping their status as gods. Both Jesus and Krishna were known as "the seed of the women bruising the serpent's head".

St. Augustine of Hippo (354-430 AD) once wrote, "This, in our day, is the Christian religion, not as having been unknown in former times, but as having recently received that name." It is absolutely ludicrous to specify that all languages come from the same Aryan source when the time that they received their new language was the same time they received their new god.

The star that appears for Jesus is the same star that appears for Krishna and all of the other saviors that mark the destruction that is used to keep secret the intensions of this organization. You can trace its appearance and the destruction of man all the way back to the enslavement of the people of Africa by the tribe of Zeus in the age of the Twins. Their legend for that age states that they "went into battle with the ape-man" When "the Great War star appeared in the sky" (see "Indaba My Children, by Zulu medicine man Credo Vusamazulu Mutwa).

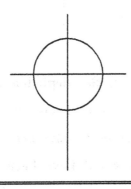

The symbol that was displayed on the previous page is the Aryan symbol of star worship; it is part of a key that has always been used by the descendants of Zeus to not only play the roll of god in the deciding of who lives or dies, but it is also the symbol that is used to keep track of the enslavement of mankind. This exact same symbol can be traced all the way back to before the age of the flood as the symbol held by the Aryans. It can be found among the oldest caves and temples of India, surrounded by what is said to be the un deciphered language that was used before these Aryans assigned Sanskrit to the slaves of the new age. When it is added to the other astrological symbols left by the descendants of Ea, you get the story that you are being told, the story that made god, god, the true story of creation.

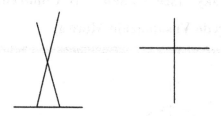

In the time of Christ, the depiction that you see illustrated above on the left would have been the easiest most efficient way for someone to have been punished for their crimes. Two boards could have been roughly cut, nailed, or even tied together at the center, then placed in the ground for immediate use. This did not happen; instead the depiction on the right was used. These boards not only had to be precisely cut to equal the measurements of a cross, but they also had to be notches so that when the boards were fastened together and placed in the ground, the weight and struggle of the man who was being placed on them would not make the upper board tilt to one side or the other. This special design was specifically crafted to represent the cross of the zodiac for the purpose of sacrificing these people to the sun. Now although the followers of this cult thought that this was absurd, this is the same story that was told in the Aztec pyramids about what was being done to Ea's people. There was no record anywhere on earth that describes the people of the serpent sacrificing anyone to the sun; in fact they reside on the most populated area of the world. That does not happen by killing off your own people.

Matthew 10:34-35 "Do not think that I have come to bring peace on earth; I have not come to bring peace, but a sword. For I have come to set a man against his father, and a daughter against her mother, and a daughter-in-law against her mother-in-law; and a man's foes will be those of his own household."

Besides the fact that the followers claim "this is not my god", the barbaric and brutal mentality of the Aryan

151

"cult of Sin" is what led them to be the rulers of the fourth world. No one would have worshipped their new god in the beginning of this new age, if they were not forced to upon the promise of death to them and their children. By the time it reached the year that I lived, this was almost completely forgotten, their censoring of what the people were allowed to know led them to believe that the word sin actually meant that they did something against god, it did not. The word sin was derived from the son of Enlil/Zeus, who would sacrifice to the sun, the people who did not obey their laws. In the bible it actually stated for the age that sin lived, Genesis 4:6 "Why are you angry? The Lord (Enlil) asked. Why is your face so dark with rage? (7) It can be bright with joy if you will do what you should! But if you refuse to (obey), watch out. Sin is waiting to attack you, longing to destroy you".

The descendants of Sin put in place the laws of this fourth world just like it was done in the time of Atlantis in Plato's dialogues. The difference was, they were not to be given out to be abided by the people who only resided in the part of the world allotted to Zeus, they were using the slaves of their religious system to force them onto the entire world. See the bible, Romans 13:1 "Everyone must submit himself to the governing authorities, for there is no authority except that which God has established. The authorities that exist

152

have been established by God. (2) Consequently, he who rebels against the authority is rebelling against what God has instituted, and those who do so will bring judgment on themselves. (3) For rulers hold no terror for those who do right, but for those who do wrong."

"Do you want to be free from fear of the one in authority? Then do what is right and he will commend you. (4) For he is God's servant to do you good. But if you do wrong, be afraid, for he does not bear the sword for nothing. He is God's servant, an agent of wrath to bring punishment on the wrongdoer."

It is in this age that we were first able to understand who the people of Tiahuanaco were referring to when they described the angelic warriors. It is in the age in which I lived that the secret organization known as the freemasons first emerged as the Knights templar. They were sent out to destroy and or burn all of the history of our past that they could get their hands on. That especially meant anyone who had any knowledge of the "foreign gods", Ea's descendants, or their teachings. Those who did were often sacrificed, many as burnt offerings. The term that was used was, "burned at the steak". They did these things to insure that we would never have the knowledge that they had, they purposely kept us ignorant.

Devices that were later found, such as the Antikythera mechanism, more than proved this fact. The fact that they were keeping secrets of enormous value from the rest of the world, knowledge that the people in my field could only imagine. The Antikythera mechanism was an ancient mechanical zodiac designed to calculate the astronomical positions of the sky at any given point in time. It was discovered off of the coast of the Greek island of Antikythera, between Kythera and Crete, in 1901. The dating of the making of this mechanical zodiac is believed to have been between 150 and 100 BC, and it is believed to have been on its way to Rome.

The strange thing was, devices like this were not seen again until almost 2000 years later, toward the end of the new age. Within 150 years of this supposedly newly discovered gear making system, we had electricity, airplanes, cars, TV, radio, to many things to mention for such a short period of time. 10,000 years ago, we had horses and wagons, 150 years before all these inventions, we still had the same thing and again, most of the people never even thought that this was odd. If they would have just checked, they would have known that these people were hoarding the knowledge and using it to play god.

The most widely circulated bible of my time was the King James Version, the King James Version was written by a 33rd degree mason. The Mormons were started by a 33rd degree mason. Jehovah's Witness were started by a 33rd degree mason, etc., etc. The masons were a branch of the Knight's Templar of the Roman Catholic Church of which could be traced back to the building of the first temples and cities described in the rig Vedas.

The small percentage of people that tried to educate themselves outside of their cities, I would estimate to be around 10 to 15%. The rest of them actually would debate on which of these branches of religion they should worship. It was this system that they had created that kept them at the status of god. Once you were surrounded by it, it wrapped a hold and would not leave you alone. You needed their money to eat, you needed their land to live, and you needed their god so that you would have a place to go when you died.

Once you were in, if you tried to escape, you were to expect the punishment of god. Exodus 20:5 "You shall not bow down to them or worship them; for I, the LORD your God, am a jealous God, punishing the children for the sin of the fathers to the third and fourth generation of those who hate me." The wrath that gods so called angelic warriors laid forth on mankind for the study of Ea's teachings plummeted the world into the modern day dark ages, this one lasted until around 1000 A.D.

One of the first things recorded after the ending of the dark ages was the first Christian crusades. It began in 1095 to rid the holy land of the followers of the age of the Ram, the slaves of the previous age. This happened to the Jews because they were not aware of this system and how it worked. When the new god was appointed, they did not want to accept it. They were left behind, just like the people of India. None of the people who worshipped the god of the previous age new how this system worked until they got to the end of the age, until then they did what they were told in the name of the god of the age that they lived.

By the time that I was born into this age, it was common knowledge that the Christian branch of this organization had been responsible for the deaths of more people than any other human force on earth, they just did not know why. Many were even in denial because their god was the new god, he died for their sins, he was their hero and he was going to return at the end to save them from the horrible events that were going to come upon the earth. They actually convinced these people that they should do nothing to save their family. They actually convinced them that they were to stand there and die because that was the way god wanted it.

The fact of the matter was, the only thing that the descendants of god wanted, was to keep their status as gods.

The only way that they could do that, was to make sure that only their descendants would live. That was the plan, that was what was supposed to be the true heaven. When they hide from the destruction, all of the noisy people would die and be out of their way.

In the original texts, like the Epic of Gilgamesh, stolen and altered for the bible of the slaves of the descendants of Zeus, it was the reason for the flood, to kill all of the noisy people. Noah was originally a follower of Ea/Poseidon, which is how he lived through the flood. Ea not only told him when the disaster was going to occur, but he also told him that he should build a boat. After surviving the flood and Enlil/Zeus finds out, it states "Just then Enlil arrived. He saw the boat and became furious, he was filled with rage at the Igigi gods, "Where did a living being escape? No man was to survive the annihilation!" This cycle that you are being told about in this book is even mentioned in this epic when it states, "They established Death and Life, but they did not make known the days of death".

These descendants of Enlil/Zeus altered these stories for the modern bible and based their strategy of destruction on not being able to trace them back. By the time of the years that I lived, they censored everything, the TV, the news, they always claimed that god was good, almost every show had at least one scene were someone was thanking

157

god. If you were not informed and educated from the outside, you would never even begin to know where to look to find out how this all came to be. One of the first clues that I was able to locate was the fact that Poseidon married a mortal; this broke the bloodline of the gods. Zeus married his sister and their bloodline remained pure all throughout history. During the time of the dark ages, the twelve tribes of the bible were still going strong. Half of the tribe was referred to as the Vikings, a tall red or blond haired people with blue eyes and beards. They whore a helmet with horns, just like the one worn by Enlil.

They were the sea branch of the 12 tribes of Zeus. The word Viking was Roman for 6 kings; the other six were land tribes such as the Norsemen. Together they were assigned to ravage plunder and rob all that they could to not only destroy their recorded presence in the previous age, but also to acquire the land from the weak for the purpose of accomplishing their goal. During the end of the medieval era around 800AD-1100AD., the Villages that were on or near any coast lived in fear of their attacks, which were often staged so that it would appear that the other tribes would win in the name of their god, the son, Jesus Christ. The people who would then be in fear of the barbaric return of this savage tribe of Vikings would then gladly hand over control of their land; they would gladly accept their religion and monetary system due to the fact that the Christian god had saved their families.

The countries that were most affected by these tactics were Scotland, Ireland, France, and England. After the tribes in the north, the Norseman, gained control of the territory of Normandy, the newly assigned Duke of Normandy, under the command of Pope Alexander 2nd, invaded England and won the Battle of Hastings in 1066 against King Harold. After this, he was given the title William I of England or William the Conqueror. He was King of England from 1066 until 1087.

After this take over, the Vikings were called back, the dark ages ended, and the territories of England were assigned a system of banking that can be traced back to the sea shells of the sea people that lived before the time of the flood. In 1844, Benjamin Disraeli, first Prime Minister of England, in a novel he published called "Coningsby, the New Generation", stated, "The world is governed by very different personages from what is imagined by those who are not behind the scenes."

William the Conqueror had kept the pure bloodline by marrying his cousin Matilda of Flanders around 1050 or 1051, he died after falling off a horse, and was then succeeded by his son William II. By 1199 under the rule of King John, England was not only bankrupt but it owed an incredibly large sum of money to the Vatican. Before their system of money, everyone there was happy; they owned their own land and paid no taxes.

Once these people were indebted, starving, and in the need to save their families, they could then easily be recruited into their almost never ending war against the descendants of Ea and their territory. A good example happened in 1521 when the tribe of Zeus sent out an expedition to destroy the Great Pyramid of the Aztec culture. No one was supposed to ever know the truth of why they were built or what the writings in them explained, and they used the same tactics that they did before the flood; they claimed these people practiced the practices of the Devil.

The expedition was assigned by the Roman Catholic Church to be carried out by the Spanish conquistador Hernán Cortés. These people not only burned and destroyed every written record that they could find in this temple, but they destroyed the entire Aztec empire. Because of their censoring of information, most of the people of my time never figured out that this was just another sacrifice of a branch of Ea's descendants to Zeus. It was one of the last remaining untouched preserving temples of the ancestors of the Hopi, and the knowledge of the tree of life that they were giving to the people to help them remember the story

160

of creation. Do not think for a second that it is a coincidence that in Spanish, the spelling of Jesus is pronounced Hey Zeus.

When the Gregorian calendar was put in place around a year later by Pope Gregory XIII, on the 24th of February 1582, it was designed around the true bloodline of the god Zeus. It started with the birth of the new god Jesus as the year 0. Offspring of the tribes on land such as Julius Caesar, became July, while Augustus Caesar became August. Descendants of the 6 kings at Sea, (the Vikings) such as Tiw, Odin, Thor & Frig became Tuesday, Wednesday, Thursday & Friday.

The oldest living descendant of this god in the time that I lived was the queen of England, and almost all of the control of money, weapons, and religion, were still in their hands. It was this system that they used to get the people to help them build the new Atlantis on part of the new world now known as the Americas. Despite their claims of new discovery, researchers like me knew they were here long before because of the artifacts they left behind. One of the most resent was the Kensington Stone. It was discovered in Kensington, Minnesota in 1898, and on it was written an inscription left by Norsemen describing their expedition into part of North America.

Manly P. Hall once stated, "The bold resolution was made that this western continent should become the sight of the philosophic empire. Just when this was done it is impossible now to say, but certainly the decision was reached prior to the time of Plato, for a thinly veiled statement of this resolution is the substance of his treaties on the Atlantic islands."

This then led to another great slaughter of the descendants of Ea as they took the land that was referred to as the New World (America) from Native Americans such as the Hopi. After these natives taught them how to grow the food needed to survive in this area, they were then slaughtered in the name of god because they were practicing the works of the devil; they were the descendants of the serpent, Ea/Poseidon, in the Garden of Eden, the god who wanted man to be like him.

After this territory was established, the city state of Washington D.C. became their new branch for weapons. It remained the dominant source of weaponry throughout the entire remaining time of the fourth world. This should have come to no surprise to the self educated because the establishers of this country were the descendants of the god Zeus. They always had the best weapons because the knowledge of the making of weapons was forbidden to everybody except the descendants of the god Zeus. This city

162

state was one of only three in the world that were established. It paid no taxes, had its own flag, and operated under Roman laws as it handed down the ones that were to be abided by the people who inhabited the surrounding territories.

In "The Secret Teachings of All Ages", 33rd degree freemason Manly P. Hall, stated, "Not only were many of the founders of the United States government Masons, but they received aid from a secret and august body existing in Europe which helped them to establish this country for a peculiar and particular purpose known only to the initiated few."

The place that controlled their system of money was known as the inner city of London, it was located in Europe. It was originally founded by the Romans in 43 AD as the town of Londinium, it operated under their laws, had its own flag, and paid no taxes. The only other place in the world where these same rules applied was their branch of religion located within the city of Rome. This city state had its own flag, paid no taxes, and operated under Roman laws. The people who were smart enough to figure this out referred to the 3 as "The Empire of the City", the rest either never new, or remained in complete denial.

These three places were where they placed the three most important Zodiac symbols of the world, the obelisks.

Two of them were part of the sun dials of the largest zodiac calendars ever known to be built. One was taken out of Egypt and constructed in St. Peters square in Rome. It was placed so that every pope that addressed the square had to face it, at the top was placed the zodiac cross.

Another one known as Cleopatra's needle was transported from Egypt and placed in the inner city of London, the headquarters of the worldwide English freemasons. The third obelisk, known as the Washington monument, was dedicated by the freemason grand lodge of the District of Columbia, in honor of the first president and freemason, George Washington. It was designed to stand 555.5 feet tall (6,666 inches) with each side being 55.5 feet wide (666 inches). 666 was the number of the sun in the forbidden Christian math known as Gematria. This obelisk was placed just as the popes in front of the white house so that every president that addressed the square had to face it.

It was dedicated to George Washington because he was the first one to ensure the enslavement of the people of the new world by implementing their system of money. In all of the text books assigned to the children to learn, he was portrayed as one of the greatest presidents of America, in reality, he was the first traitor. It is during his term that the entire ground design of Washington D.C. was built around the symbol of Athena, the daughter of Zeus. This Masonic symbol was so large; it could only be seen from the air. The common people had no idea that it was even there. At the main point of this star existed the White house, not far from it was the Capital building, it had on top a statue of Athena with a scroll that read E Pluribus Unum "one from many". In reverse it meant "many from one" because she seeded all of their families.

These same designs were assigned to our currency; on the back of the dollar bill they put the seal containing the eagle, the symbol of Zeus. It was the symbol that was also assigned to the country and in its beak there was the same scroll reading E Pluribus Unum, "one from many", "many from one". On the other seal was placed the pyramid of Egypt, the first territory to be taken from the descendants of Ea/Poseidon. Above it said Annuit Coeptis meaning "he has favored our undertakings". In the middle of the bill it stated "in god we trust"

By drawing a line in the pyramid seal from the A in Annuit, to the S in Coeptis, the line being the same length as the bottom of the pyramid. Then down to a point where the second O is in Ordo, you would have an upside down pyramid. If you were to write down the letters at each of the six points, it spelled out the word mason. Then when you drew a line to connect the letters that spelled out the word mason, starting at M to A to O to S to N, and back to M, you had the inverted pentagram, the symbol of Athena.

A. Ralph Epperson once stated: "All the staff officers (George) Washington trusted were Masons and all the leading generals of the Army were Masons."

All major corporations in America were run by the descendants of these masons. Almost all of the controlling corporations had Masonic symbols in their logos. A good example was Time Warner cable and the eye of Horus. That was our major source for the common people to get their information from TV. On the internet, the first source for information was yet again the eye of Horus and AOL. President Woodrow Wilson once stated, "Some of the biggest men in the United States, in the field of commerce and manufacture, are afraid of something. They know that there is a power somewhere so organized, so subtle, so watchful, so interlocked, so complete, so pervasive, that they had better not speak above their breath when they speak in condemnation of it." Whatever they wanted the people of the fourth world to know or learn was all decided by these people.

In a book titled "Tragedy and Hope: A History of the World in Our Time" Professor Carroll Quigley of Georgetown University stated, "The powers of financial capitalism had another far reaching aim, nothing less than to create a world system of financial control in private hands able to dominate the political system of each country and the economy of the world as a whole. This system was to be controlled in a feudalist fashion by the central banks of the world acting in concert, by secret agreements, arrived at in frequent private meetings and conferences. The apex of the system was the Bank for International Settlements in Basle, Switzerland, a private bank owned and controlled by the worlds' central banks which were themselves private corporations. The growth of financial capitalism made possible a centralization of world economic control and use of this power for the direct benefit of financiers and the indirect injury of all other economic groups."

All of the religions mentioned in this book were still awaiting their savior when I wrote it. The followers were completely unaware that he was never going to come because they were appointed these gods so that they could be used to bring about a battle that was to take place during the end of the fourth world.

One of the most well known of the freemasons for the time of the savior was Albert pike. Pike was said to be so high up in this secret organization that he had a bracelet that let him keep in constant contact with the one in which he was getting his orders. This was in a time where the concept of a communication bracelet was unheard of, 100 years later, that type of communication wasn't given a second thought, everyone could obtain it.

During his time, Pike handed over a plan that was to be used to enslave the rest of the world; it was very similar to the plan that was used to start the war with the descendants of Ea. According to documents, Albert Pike stated, "The First World War must be brought about in order to permit the Illuminati to overthrow the power of the Czars in Russia and of making that country a fortress of atheistic Communism. The divergences caused by the "agentur" (agents) of the Illuminati between the British and Germanic Empires will be used to foment this war. At the end of the war, Communism will be built and used in order to destroy the other governments and in order to weaken the religions."

This happened just as it was written, and was brought about by the alliance that Albert Pike had made with Otto von Bismarck between 1871 and 1898. This political alliances of England on one side, and Germany on the other, was the reason behind the First World War. In 1941, British military historian Major General J.F.C. Fuller stated on the subject, "The government of the Western nations, whether monarchical or republican, had passed into the invisible hands of a plutocracy, international in power and grasp. It was, I venture to suggest, this semioccult power which....pushed the mass of the American people into the cauldron of World War I."

Pike stated for the second, "The Second World War must be fomented by taking advantage of the differences between the Fascists and the political Zionists. This war must be brought about so that Nazism is destroyed and that the political Zionism be strong enough to institute a sovereign state of Israel in Palestine. During the Second World War, International Communism must become strong enough in order to balance Christendom, which would be then restrained and held in check until the time when we would need it for the final social cataclysm."

In February of 1933, a man known as Hitler used the same tactic that was used against the people of Ea. He staged an attack by burning down his own parliament building, the Reichstag; he then blamed it on communist terrorists. This allowed him to pass the Enabling Act, destroying the German constitution. In addressing this incident he stated, "an evil exists that threatens every man, woman and child of this great nation, we must take steps to ensure our domestic security and protect our homeland".

Not since the Native Americans were exterminated in the beginning of the invasion of the new world (America) was one race of people burned and tortured in such a short

169

period of time. These people were the Jews, the slaves of the previous age. This was the same thing the bible states was done to the people that were still worshipping the "Bull" of the age before. And they did this task while using a substance made from the same ingredients as Soma, the drink described in the Rig-Veda. Adolph Hitler stated on this, "I believe today that my conduct is in accordance with the will of the Almighty Creator." At another time he stated, "Who says I am not under the special protection of God?"

The result of this Second World War made the enforcers of Communism so strong that they began taking over weaker governments. In 1945, at the Potsdam Conference between Truman, Churchill, and Stalin, a large section of Europe was simply just handed over to Russia with no questions asked. Franklin D. Roosevelt, 33rd Degree Freemason and President of the United States once stated: "... in politics nothing is accidental. If something happens, be assured it was planned this way."

In September of 2001, two buildings that were commonly used to represent America were hit by two planes and collapsed. The attack was quickly blamed on Muslim terrorists; the Muslim religion that was started by the descendants of the followers of Zeus in the age of the Ram. In a speech given by President George Bush, he stated, "an evil exists that threatens every man, woman and child of this great nation, we must take steps to ensure our domestic security and protect our homeland". It was almost the same exact speech that was given by Hitler. The people were outraged, and they quickly voted in laws that altered the constitution. They made it so their own phones could be tapped, their own homes could be entered without warrants, and anyone they wanted in this so called free nation could be dragged away, tortured, and held indefinitely without ever having to be given a reason why.

Anybody with any knowledge of the history of the earths past new how ignorant these people were, there was no way that it was a coincidence that almost 6,000 years to the date of the last global disaster, almost all modern inventions just suddenly emerged onto the scene, again. There was no way that almost exactly on the date 2000 of the new calendar year marking the 6,000 year anniversary of their last staged airplane attack on the descendants of Ea that they accidentally printed a new twenty dollar bill, that with three folds, could be folded into a plane that represented every event that took place the following year.

Bills 5, 10, 20, 50 and 100, when folded like this plane, actually showed a cartoon depiction of these two buildings catching fire, and collapsing. Around the nose of this folded paper plane, it actually read "in god we trust". If you did the same thing to the dollar bill, it showed the eagle as ruler over the pyramid of Egypt, the one that contained the "key of life", the one that was built in honor of the coming together of the three races.

The two buildings that collapsed were paid for to be built by a group of masons that were not only in charge of almost all of the decisions of the country, but they had previously begun to openly use the term "New World Order". I am not going to go into much detail of this because I was able to uncover so much information about the roll they played in the fourth world, I wrote it into a book titled "OLD WORLD SECRETS THE OMEGA PROJECT CODES", I considered this book to be the New Testament of the things that were done.

33rd degree Freemason, Manly P. Hall once stated, "Many of these ancient cults vanished from the Earth without revealing their secrets, but a few have survived the test of ages and their mysteries' symbols are still preserved. Much of the ritualism of Freemasonry is based on the trials to which candidates were subjected by the ancient hierophants before the keys of wisdom (life) were entrusted to them."

The main people behind the building of the towers that collapsed were the Rockefellers. Congressman Larry P. McDonald stated in 1976 that, "The drive of the

172

Rockefellers and their allies is to create a one-world government combining super capitalism and Communism under the same tent, all under their control.... Do I mean conspiracy? Yes I do. I am convinced there is such a plot, international in scope, generations old in planning, and incredibly evil in intent..." He was killed not long after when his flight, a Korean Airline 747, was shot down by the soviets.

Ten years before these twin towers collapsed, David Rockefeller, founder of the Trilateral Commission, in an address to a meeting of The Trilateral Commission, stated in June, 1991, "We are grateful to The Washington Post, The New York Times, Time Magazine, and other great publications whose directors have attended our meetings and respected their promises of discretion for almost forty years. It would have been impossible for us to develop our plan for the world if we had been subject to the bright lights of publicity during those years. But, the work is now much more sophisticated and prepared to march towards a world government. The supranational sovereignty of an intellectual elite and world bankers is surely preferable to the national auto determination practiced in past centuries."

When I traced it back, I found that the talk of this "New World Order" first came on the scene around the same time of the emergence of all of the new great inventions. Around this same time, all of the news reporting agencies that were not owned by this organization was purchased. In 1917 congressman Oscar Callaway stated, "An agreement was reached; the policy of the papers was bought, to be paid for by the month; an editor was furnished for each paper to properly supervise and edit information regarding the questions of preparedness, militarism, financial policies, and other things of national and international nature considered vital to the interests of the purchasers."

Mention of the New World Order, oldest to newest

In an address delivered before the Union League of Philadelphia, Nov. 27, 1915, Nicholas Murray Butler stated, "The old world order changed when this war-storm broke. The old international order passed away as suddenly, as unexpectedly, and as completely as if it had been wiped out by a gigantic flood, by a great tempest, or by a volcanic eruption. The old world order died with the setting of that day's sun and a new world order is being born while I speak, with birth-pangs so terrible that it seems almost incredible that life could come out of such fearful suffering and such overwhelming sorrow."

174

M. C. Alexander, Executive Secretary of the American Association for International Conciliation, in a subscription letter for the periodical International Conciliation 1919, "The peace conference has assembled. It will make the most momentous decisions in history, and upon these decisions will rest the stability of the new world order and the future peace of the world."

Dr. Augustus O. Thomas, president of the World Federation of Education Associations, August 1927 stated, "If there are those who think we are to jump immediately into a new world order, actuated by complete understanding and brotherly love, they are doomed to disappointment. If we are ever to approach that time, it will be after patient and persistent effort of long duration. The present international situation of mistrust and fear can only be corrected by a formula of equal status, continuously applied, to every phase of international contacts, until the cobwebs of the old order are brushed out of the minds of the people of all lands."

H. G. Wells, in his book entitled "The New World Order", published in 1939, stated, "when the struggle seems to be drifting definitely towards a world social democracy, there may still be very great delays and disappointments before it becomes an efficient and beneficent world system. Countless people ... will hate the new world order ... and will die protesting against it. When we attempt to evaluate its promise, we have to bear in mind the distress of a generation or so of malcontents, many of them quite gallant and graceful-looking people."

In an excerpt from A Memorial to be Addressed to the House of Bishops and the House of Clerical and Lay Deputies of the Protestant Episcopal Church in General Convention, October 1940, "The term Internationalism has been popularized in recent years to cover an interlocking financial, political, and economic world force for the purpose of establishing a World Government. Today Internationalism is heralded from pulpit and platform as a 'League of Nations' or a 'Federated Union' to which the United States must surrender a definite part of its National Sovereignty. The World Government plan is being advocated under such alluring names as the 'New International Order,' 'The New World Order,' 'World Union Now,' 'World Commonwealth of Nations,' 'World Community,' etc. All the terms have the same objective; however, the line of approach may be religious or political according to the taste or training of the individual."

Title of article in "The Tablet", Brooklyn, March 1942 "New World Order Needed for Peace: State Sovereignty Must Go, Declares Notre Dame Professor"

176

American Institute of Judaism, excerpt from article in "The New York Times", December 1942, "The statement went on to say that the spiritual teachings of religion must become the foundation for the new world order and that national sovereignty must be subordinate to the higher moral law of God."

Norman Thomas stated in his book "What Is Our Destiny", 1944, "There are some plain common-sense considerations applicable to all these attempts at world planning. They can be briefly stated: 1. To talk of blueprints for the future or building a world order is, if properly understood, suggestive, but it is also dangerous. Societies grow far more truly than they are built. A constitution for a new world order is never like a blueprint for a skyscraper."

In an excerpt from an article by Ralph W. Page in "The Philadelphia Bulletin", May 1944, "He [John Foster Dulles] stated directly to me that he had every reason to believe that the Governor [Thomas E. Dewey of New York] accepts his point of view and that he is personally convinced that this is the policy that he would promote with great vigor if elected. So it is fair to say that on the first round the Sphinx of Albany has established himself as a prima facie champion of a strong and definite new world order."

"The New York Times", February 1962, "The United Nations, he told an audience at Harvard University, 'has not been able--nor can it be able--to shape a new world order which events so compellingly demand.' ... The new world order that will answer economic, military, and political problems, he said, 'urgently requires, I believe, that the United States take the leadership among all free peoples to make the underlying concepts and aspirations of national sovereignty truly meaningful through the federal approach."

Richard Nixon stated in "Foreign Affairs, October 1967, "The developing coherence of Asian regional thinking is reflected in a disposition to consider problems and loyalties in regional terms, and to evolve regional approaches to development needs and to the evolution of a new world order."

In an excerpt from an article in "The New York Times", February 1972, "He [President Nixon] spoke of the talks as a beginning, saying nothing more about the prospects for future contacts and merely reiterating the belief he brought to China that both nations share an interest in peace and building a new world order."

CFR member Richard Gardner, writing in the April 1974 issue of the CFR's journal, "Foreign Affairs", "The New

World Order will have to be built from the bottom up rather than from the top down...but in the end run around national sovereignty, eroding it piece by piece will accomplish much more than the old fashioned frontal assault."

In August 1975, Arthur Schlesinger Jr., The CFR Journal Foreign Affairs stated, "We are not going to achieve a New World Order without paying for it in blood as well as in words and money."

Richard A. Falk, in an article entitled "Toward a New World Order: Modest Methods and Drastic Visions," in the book "On the Creation of a Just World Order", 1975, "The existing order is breaking down at a very rapid rate, and the main uncertainty is whether mankind can exert a positive role in shaping a new world order or is doomed to await collapse in a passive posture. We believe a new order will be born no later than early in the next century and that the death throes of the old and the birth pangs of the new will be a testing time for the human species."

Henry Kissinger, in address before the General Assembly of the United Nations, October 1975, "My country's history, Mr. President, tells us that it is possible to fashion unity while cherishing diversity, that common action is possible despite the variety of races, interests, and beliefs we see here in this chamber. Progress and peace and justice are attainable. So we say to all peoples and governments: Let us fashion together a new world order."

This is part of article in "The New York Times, November 1975, "At the old Inter-American Office in the Commerce Building here in Roosevelt's time, as Assistant Secretary of State for Latin American Affairs under President Truman, as chief whip with Adlai Stevenson and Tom Finletter at the founding of the United Nations in San Francisco, Nelson Rockefeller was in the forefront of the struggle to establish not only an American system of political and economic security but a new world order."

In June, 1977, the title of an article on commencement address at the University of Pennsylvania by Hubert H. Humphrey, printed in the Pennsylvania Gazette, read "A New World Order"

Mikhail Gorbachev, in an address at the United Nations, December 1988, "Further global progress is now possible only through a quest for universal consensus in the movement towards a new world order."

Richard Gephardt, in "The Wall Street Journal", September 1990, "We can see beyond the present shadows of war in the Middle East to a new world order where the strong work together to deter and stop aggression."

President George Bush, January 1991, "If we do not follow the dictates of our inner moral compass and stand up for human life, then his lawlessness will threaten the peace and democracy of the emerging new world order we now see, this long dreamed-of vision we've all worked toward for so long."

An excerpt from A. M. Rosenthal, in "The New York Times", January 1991, "But it became clear as time went on that in Mr. Bush's mind the New World Order was founded on a convergence of goals and interests between the U.S. and the Soviet Union, so strong and permanent that they would work as a team through the U.N. Security Council."

George McGovern, in "The New York Times", February 1991, "I would support a Presidential candidate who pledged to take the following steps: ... At the end of the war in the Persian Gulf, press for a comprehensive Middle East settlement and for a 'new world order' based not on Pax Americana but on peace through law with a stronger U.N. and World Court."

William Safire, in "The New York Times", February 1991, "... it's Bush's baby, even if he shares its popularization with Gorbachev. Forget the Hitler 'new order' root; F.D.R. used the phrase earlier."

Brent Scowcroft, August 1990, quoted in "The Washington Post", May 1991, "We believe we are creating the beginning of a new world order coming out of the collapse of the U.S.-Soviet antagonisms."

An article by Sen. Joseph R. Biden, Jr. in "The Wall Street Journal", April 1992, "How I Learned to Love the New World Order"

Title of a book excerpt by Henry Kissinger, in "Time Magazine", March 1994, "How to Achieve The New World Order"

This is part of full-page advertisement by the government of Morocco in "The New York Times", April 1994, "The Final Act of the Uruguay Round, marking the conclusion of the most ambitious trade negotiation of our century, will give birth - in Morocco - to the World Trade Organization, the third pillar of the New World Order, along with the United Nations and the International Monetary Fund."

The title of an article by Kenichi Ohmae, political reform leader in Japan, in "The Wall Street Journal"

1994, "New World Order: The Rise of the Region-
e"

Nelson Mandela, in "The Philadelphia Inquirer", October 1994, "The new world order that is in the making must focus on the creation of a world of democracy, peace and prosperity for all."

An article by Stephen John Stedman in Foreign Affairs, May/June 1995, "Alchemy for a New World Order"

"New World Order" hand sign description

The same type of sign that represented Zeus, all throughout the ages of his power, was the same type of sign that was used to represent the "New World Order". It was done by making a relaxed fist, then pointing straight out your pinky and index finger. Now when you look at the side of your hand, with your middle finger following from the point around to the point of the index finger, you will see the letter N which stands for (New). Then when you look with the pinky and index facing you, it is the letter W, which stands for (World). Then when you turn back to the side and view your thumb touching your middle finger, it is the letter O, which stands for (Order).

Albert Pike stated for the third world war, "The Third World War must be fomented by taking advantage of the differences caused by the "agentur" of the "Illuminati" between the political Zionists and the leaders of Islamic World. The war must be conducted in such a way that Islam (the Moslem Arabic World) and political Zionism (the State of Israel) mutually destroy each other. Meanwhile the other nations, once more divided on this issue will be constrained to fight to the point of complete physical, moral, spiritual and economical exhaustion...We shall unleash the Nihilists and the atheists, and we shall provoke a formidable social cataclysm which in all its horror will show clearly to the nations the effect of absolute atheism, origin of savagery and of the most bloody turmoil."

"Then everywhere, the citizens, obliged to defend themselves against the world minority of revolutionaries, will exterminate those destroyers of civilization, and the multitude, disillusioned with Christianity, whose deistic spirits will from that moment be without compass or direction, anxious for an ideal, but without knowing where to render its adoration, will receive the true light through

184

the universal manifestation of the pure doctrine of Lucifer, brought finally out in the public view. This manifestation will result from the general reactionary movement which will follow the destruction of Christianity and atheism, both conquered and exterminated at the same time."

Myron Fagan stated on the subject, "The idea was that those who direct the overall conspiracy could use the differences in those two so-called ideologies [marxism/fascism/socialism v. democracy/ capitalism] to enable them [the Illuminati] to divide larger and larger portions of the human race into opposing camps so that they could be armed and then brainwashed into fighting and destroying each other." Albert Pike was a known racist and traitor to the United States, his statue was erected in Washington D.C. as one of the most important people in American history.

Chapter 9

The Last Supper

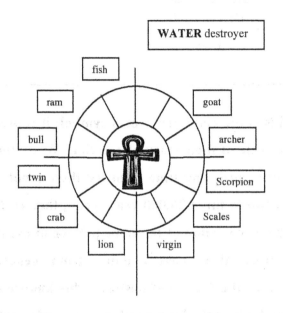

The Hopi claim for the age of the water bearer, if man does not cooperate with Masaw (the Masons), and the laws of the creator, there will be a takeover of the earth by him (them). They say for this time that represents the age of the destroyer, when the earth goes out of balance, Masaw will attempt to re-balance it, but it will cause great destruction.

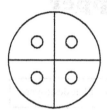

This is the Hopi new world symbol; it represents the complete cycle of their story of creation. When the ancient keepers of records and time recorded these events over the period of two to three 26,000 year cycles, they realized that the earth always followed the same pattern of events. These records were then passed down from generation to generation as the "tablet of destiny", this knowledge made the descendants of the keepers of these records, gods.

Luke 22:10 "and he replied, "As soon as you enter Jerusalem, you will see a man walking along carrying a pitcher of water. Follow him into the house he enters." This was the last supper, the representation of the end of the age of Pisces, the beginning of the age of the water bearer.

The age of the water bearer was referred to by different names all around the world, such as "Judgment Day," "The End of this Creation," "The End of Time as We Know it," "The Time of Trial on Earth," "The Shift of the

Ages", "The Time of Great Purification" and simply Revelation, just to name a few.

The last time we entered the age of the water bearer was the last time that Neanderthal man ever walked the face of the earth. The youngest Neanderthal finds are Hyaena Den in the UK, and the Vindija found in Croatia, both estimated to be around thirty thousand years old. No Neanderthal remains have ever been found living past the age of the destroyer, 26,000 years ago.

At the time that I wrote this book, the population of the planet was increasing by 216,000 people per day, as of March of 2009, the total population was estimated to be 6.77 billion people. Of this total, 33.32% were estimated to be Christians (of which Roman Catholics 16.99%, Protestants 5.78%, Orthodox 3.53%, Anglicans 1.25%), Muslims 21.01%, Hindus 13.26%, and Jews 0.23%. None of which had any clue as to when they should expect the return of their messiah, they had no clue because their god had never told them about the "tree of life".

In the Mayan texts that escaped the burning and destruction brought on by the church, they refer to this cycle of the Zodiac that you are reading about in this book as the "Yaxche", the "tree of life". These records in these temples were not prophecies, these people knew about the true story of creation and how to prepare their families for

189

survival, the god Zeus took that away from us. The date in which the Mayan entered the present world was August 13, 3113 BC., the age they refer to as the time of the great flood. In Mayan long count notation, this was written as 13.0.0.0.0., and is referred to as the Age of the Fifth Sun.

Dr. Jose Arguelles stated in "Time and the Technosphere", "August 13, 3113 BC is as precise and accurate as one can get for a beginning of history: the first Egyptian dynasty is dated to ca 3100 BC; the first 'city,' Uruk, in Mesopotamia, also ca 3100 BC; the Hindu Kali Yuga, 3102 BC; and most interestingly, the division of time into 24 hours of 60 minutes each and each minute into 60 seconds [and the division of the circle into 360 degrees], also around 3100 BC, in Sumeria."

Within the 5,125 year cycle that takes place during the age of the fifth sun lies 13 smaller cycles known as the "13 Baktun Count," or the "long count". Each Baktun cycle is 394 years long, or 144,000 days. We entered the 13th Baktun cycle right after Pope Gregory XIII applied their world wide 12 month calendar system. It was said to be the final period from 1618-2012 AD., this end date was also referred to them as 13.0.0.0.0. The Maya show that at the end of this final Baktun, the water bearer appears and covers the world; they claim that it will be a time of great forgetting.

Plato stated for the events after the flood, "when you and the other nations are beginning to be provided with letters, and the other requisites of civilized life, the stream from heaven, like a pestilence, comes pouring down, and leaves only those of you who are destitute of letters and education; and so you have to begin all over again like children..."

Scholar and author John Major Jenkins stated, "On 13.0.0.0.0, the December solstice sun will be found in the band of the Milky Way. We can call this an alignment between the galactic plane and the solstice meridian. This is an event that has slowly converged over a period of thousands of years, and is caused by the precession of the equinoxes. The place where the December solstice sun crosses the Milky Way is precisely the location of the "dark-rift in the Milky Way."

Leviathan (Job 41) was the reference in the bible that was refereeing to this dark rift; it was the time that the serpent bites its own tail. I never understood until I started my research on this cycle of the zodiac, that time has a beginning and an end, an alpha and omega. The Maya, Hopi, Egyptians, Kabbalists, Essenes, Qero elders of Peru, Navajo, Cherokee, Apache, Iroquois, Dogon Tribe, Aborigines, Sumerians, Tibetans, and countless others who left this knowledge, were all descendants of Ea, they were all entrusted with a part of the "tree of life", the true story of creation.

The Hopi say that at the end of the fourth world, containers of ashes will be thrown from the sky. They say that this will cause the lands to burn and the oceans to boil. They claim that the seas will begin to rise, and great quakes will shake all corners of the earth. The time in which this is to occur is said to be shortly after the appearance of the ninth sign.

This is a list of the signs:

The First Sign sates, "the coming of the white-skinned men who took the land that was not theirs."

The Second Sign states, "Our lands will see the coming of spinning wheels filled with voices."

The Third Sign states, "A strange beast like a buffalo but with great long horns will overrun the land in large numbers."

The Fourth Sign states, "The land will be crossed by snakes of iron."

The Fifth Sign states, "The land shall be criss-crossed by a giant spider's web."

The Sixth sign states, "The land shall be criss-crossed with rivers of stone that make pictures in the sun."

192

The Seventh Sign states, "You will hear of the sea turning black, and many living things dying because of it."

The Eight Sign states, "You will see many youth come and join the tribal nations to learn their ways and wisdom.

The Ninth and Last Sign states, "You will hear of a dwelling-place in the heavens, above the earth, that shall fall with a great crash. It will appear as a blue star."

These stars are what have always been used to mark time, and the Hopi were not the only people that new of the secrets that the church was trying to hide. There are several people that I have discovered that seem to know the plans that this organization had in store for our future, they new we had already invented things such as flight.

For example, English oracle mother Shipton, who lived in Yorkshire in the early 1500's, stated "when pictures look alive with movements free, when ships like fishes swim beneath the sea. When men outstripping birds can sore the sky then half the world deep drenched in blood shall die...and lands will crack and rend anew you think it strange it will come true, and in some far off distant land some men, oh such a tiny band will have to leave their solid mount, and span the earth those few to count. Who survives this and then begin the human race again. But not on land already there but on ocean beds, stark, dry and bare. Not every soul on earth will die. As the dragons tail goes sweeping by". The entire work is encoded with astrology like the bible and the description of Leviathan is mentioned several times, his tail only goes by approximately once every 26,000 years with the passing of the age of Pisces.

Merlin the magician was considered one of Europe's finest seers in the middle ages. He was described as a Celtic shaman, half man, half demon. The name Merlin comes from an older Welsh name Myrddin. To them he was Myrddin Wyllt, meaning (Merlin the wild), or half crazed man of the forest. This is some of the things he stated, "at that time shall a man standing on the shore of England speak instantly to a man standing on the shore of France through a speaking stone. The Severn Sea shall discharge itself through seven mouths and the river Usk burn for seven months. Fishes shall die in the heat thereof and shall grow multiple tails. London shall mourn the death of 20,000 and the river Thames shall turn to blood. The cult of religion shall be destroyed completely, and the ruin of the churches shall be clear for all to see. The charioteer of York will soothe the people. He will draw his sword and threaten the east, and he will fill with blood the ruts made by his wheels. Winds shall fight together with a dreadful blast.

The castle of Venus shall be restored. Men will turn their backs on heaven and fix their eyes on the earth."

"The twelve mansions of the stars will weep to see their inmates transgress so. The Gemini (Twins) will cease their wanton embraces and will dispatch Aquarius (Water Bearer) to the fountains. The seas shall rise up in the twinkling of an eye. The moisture of the sky will cease. The planets will run riot through the signs." Again, the entire story is encoded with the stars and again a completely unrelated ancient person describes the same astrological end.

The oracle known as Sibyl is thought to have lived in a cave near modern Naples around the 6th century BC. Her predictions were written onto scrolls and put in the temple of Jupiter (temple of Zeus) as the most sacred documents of Roman religious practice. They claimed the god Apollo would take over her body and give her information, the god Apollo was the son of Zeus. They wanted the people to think that one of her greatest predictions was the coming of the new Christ; it was not a prediction at all. Michel Angelo painted her into the Sistine Chapel, which was built within the Vatican by Pope Sixtus IV. Not far from her was painted the depiction of Zeus, the Vatican openly admitted that this was a painting of god.

She claimed the world would last for nine periods of 800 years. She said the 10th would begin around 2000 AD, and stated, "these things in the 10th generation shall come to pass. The earth shall be shaken by a great earthquake that throws many cities into the sea. There shall be war; fire shall come flashing forth from the heavens, and many cities burn. Black ashes shall fill the great sky. Then know the anger of the gods".

One of the main events that should have raised red flags in the heads of researchers was the third prophecy of Fatima, from Portugal, 1917, the Vatican declared it too horrible to mention. In 1984, after almost sixty years of people begging to find out what was revealed, Pope John Paul 2nd gave a speech saying, "the catastrophic nature of the third prophecy is so great that millions of lives will be lost. There is no need to panic the world over such a great loss of life." He mentioned global tidal waves and earthquakes of terrible magnitude. But just as they have been doing for thousands of years, they lowered your chance of being able to survive by keeping when it was going to happen a secret. They knew exactly when the day was going to come; Pope John Paul 2nd was first a polish actor by the name of Karol Wojtyla.

Another one of the predictions that involved the church was St. Malachi, 11th century mystic. He claimed that

196

god showed him all of the popes that would be from his time to the last pope. This consisted of 112 Popes', with clues to the identity of each, Pope John Paul 2nd was the 110th pope. After his death in 2005, while in the process of electing the 111th pope, an article appeared out of India the day before. A man said to the cardinals, "make sure that the Pope you elect does not have anything to do with the olive, because the clue for the next pope was the glory of the olive."

When the identity of the 111 pope was exposed, they chose Cardinal Ratzinger of Germany. Everyone was happy because it had nothing to do with the olive. But when Popes are elected, they choose a name for themselves, usually something special to them. It was announced he would rule under the name Benedict 16. St. Benedict was the patron St. of Europe, he gave birth to a powerful order called the Benedictine order, in which the symbol was the olive. The Pope deliberately made this prophecy come true, just like they did with the coming of Christ.

It was things like this that made me realize that there were people behind the scenes that were deliberately making many of the events in the bible come true. The bible that was given to the people of my time was nothing more than the representation of the fourth world of this zodiac cycle. The first section, the Old Testament, was the creator, the second, the New Testament, was the savior, and the third, revelation, was the destroyer. The followers of this religion were never given any chance for survival. They simply traded the future lives of their family for a false promise of a fake paradise after their death. During the age of the savior, this organization took every dime that was given to them by these innocent people, and used it to fund the wars that they started for the purpose of insuring that they kept control of every territory that they needed to be able to survive the end of the upcoming age. They kept control of almost every place that was rumored to be the hiding places of the advanced people of the past.

If you are not sure of what I am referring, all around the world in many different cultures, they claim there are races living under the earth. Some of them even say that there are entire civilizations that can be reached by tunnel systems leading down under the earth's crust. These tunnel systems are said to crisscross in all different directions, both man made and natural. There are so many of these tunnels that there was a show on the "History Channel" called "Cities of the Underworld" that was specifically dedicated to them.

The stories of these underground cities led to a theory known as the hollow earth theory, it suggests that there is a race of people highly advanced that have always lived under the earth's surface. One of the most well known of these cities is Agharta; it is the capital city of Shamballa. According to legend it was an inner continent located just beneath the earth's crust. It is claimed that the people who went there, did so because of all of the wars and cataclysms that took place on the surface of the earth.

These are some of the caves that people have thought of as possibly being the ones that were used during these great disasters. Manaus in Brazil, the caves of Iguacu Falls, and Mount Epomeo, in Italy. The Kentucky mammoth cave in South Central Kentucky, and Mount Shasta, located in California, is said to be the location of where the Agharthean city of Telos exists underneath the surface of the mountain.

Located beneath the Mato Grosso plains of Brazil, is said to be the city of Posid. There is also an entrance located in the Himalayan Mountains of Tibet, where the underground city is called the city of Shonshe, it is said to be guarded by Hindu monks. In Mongolia, there is said to be the underground city of Shingwa, right near the border of China. And there is also said to be one located underneath the Great Pyramid of Giza in Egypt, and an entrance located in King Solomon's mines.

Not to mention there are many of these entrances said to be located around the Grand Canyon area. For example, Stanton's cave, the bad part is, it has been sealed off with bars. Another one is located at the bottom of the canyon of the little Colorado, just above its junction with the Colorado River. The entrance at this location actually looks like a giant ant hill. This place is not only thought of as a sacred place of pilgrimage for the Hopi, it is off limits to everyone except them. There is even said to be entrances at the North and South Pole.

In an article titled "Doomsday Vault Design Unveiled" written by Mark Kinver, a science and nature reporter for the BBC news, he stated, "The final design for a "doomsday" vault that will house seeds from all known varieties of food crops has been unveiled by the Norwegian government. The Svalbard International Seed Vault will be built into a mountainside on a remote island near the North Pole. The vault aims to safeguard the world's agriculture from future catastrophes, such as nuclear war, asteroid strikes and climate change." If there was a pole shift, these people would be in the middle of a fertile land with all of the seeds needed to create the new world, just like they did before.

I am absolutely convinced that the descendants of this organization have been building, and adding on to these underground safe houses, ever since mankind can remember. One of the most modern of these facilities is known by many as "The Denver International Airport" or "DIA". Many claim it is the western sector of the "New World Order" because of the fact that inside, the air port is riddled with Masonic artwork and sculptures. There are so many that it has led to the belief that it was built as a control Center for the purpose of world domination.

The dedication or Capstone to this Airport is even Masonic, there is another one located in the great hall, or south eastern side of the terminal, only it is made of granite, and the Capstone has the inscription, "New World Airport commission". It is an ideal location for such a project because the airport is located in a very high altitude, in an area that would be considered ideal for this kind of underground building; the territory is known for its underground caverns.

One of the first people to bring this airport to the attention of the public was a guy named Phil Schneider. He became a whistleblower on underground Airport facilities, and even though I try to keep as down to earth as I possibly can when reporting my finds, he was found dead with piano wire wrapped around his neck, sources claim he had been beaten severely. While alive, he claimed to have helped build the DIA and other underground facilities such as area 51 and Dulce.

This is part of a lecture he gave in May of 1995. "To give you an overview of basically what I am, I started off and went through engineering school. Half of my school was in that field, and I built up a reputation for being a geological engineer, as well as a structural engineer with both military and aerospace applications. I have helped build two main bases in the United States that have some significance as far as what is called the New World Order."

He goes on to say "Presently, there are 129 deep underground military bases in the United States. They have been building these 129 bases day and night, unceasingly, since the early 1940's. Some of them were built even earlier than that. These bases are basically large cities underground connected by high-speed magneto-leviton trains that have speeds up to Mach 2."

Inside of the Denver International Airport, in the same area as the Masonic Capstone, there are not only designs on the floor, but also there are the words DZIT DIT GAII, which means "Black Sun". All over the walls of the airport there are murals of an apocalyptic type nature. One of the murals depicts three caskets, each one containing a dead body. One of them is a black woman, another is a Jewish woman, and yet another is an American Indian woman. In this same mural is also a depiction of the destruction of cities and forests. In the city there is a little girl holding a Mayan tablet which predicts the destruction of civilization.

Another mural depicts a figure in a destroyed city wearing a gas mask. In this one there are women carrying dead babies. There is another mural with a German boy in it that is collecting from all the other children of the world, all of the world's weapons. He has a huge iron fist and is pounding all of the weapons into plowshares on an anvil. It makes me think of the Garden of Eden, and humanity starting all over again.

Other murals depict nothing but mind altering and poisonous plants and animals commonly found in Masonic practices. Phil Schneider said that during the last year he worked on construction, it was being linked to an underground base at least eight levels deep. This base was said to be a 4.5 square mile underground city. All we really need to do to find the source of such a strange design would be (follow the money) look at the people who put the system of money into place, and they just so happen to have put the same type of strange symbolism in their new IRS headquarters.

When speaking of the struggle for survival Adolph Hitler once stated, "Struggle is the father of all things. It is not by the principles of humanity that man lives or is able to preserve himself above the animal world, but solely by means of the most brutal struggle."

After these people emerge from these places, according to the bible, for the Age of Aquarius, the age of the destroyer, there will be a new name, for the new god, just as there always has been. Revelation 3:12 states, "I will write upon him My New Name". This new god will be assigned to the people that may still be left alive, along with their new language, just like what has always been done. A site found on the 33rd parallel N, the same as Iraq, verifies this fact; it is called the Georgia Guidestones. They are located in Georgia, the 13th of the 13 original Masonic colonies. This site resembles Stonehenge, not only because it was built of giant stones, but also because it is aligned to the sun.

It was built anonymously, and the only clue left was the name R.C. Christian. This in turn has led some to make the connection to the Brotherhood of the Rosy Cross and the Rosicrucian order, which is also a branch of the freemasons. Written on these stones, are 12 different languages, 8 of which are describing the 10 laws that are to be applied by the new ruler of this new age. The ten rules are found written on both sides of each of the four upright stones. Moving clockwise around the structure from due north, the languages are: English, Spanish, Swahili, Hindi, Hebrew, Arabic, ancient Chinese, and Russian.

The message in English reads:

(1) MAINTAIN HUMANITY UNDER 500,000,000
IN PERPETUAL BALANCE WITH NATURE

(2) GUIDE REPRODUCTION WISELY —
IMPROVING FITNESS AND DIVERSITY

(3) UNITE HUMANITY WITH A LIVING
NEW LANGUAGE

(4) RULE PASSION — FAITH — TRADITION
AND ALL THINGS WITH TEMPERED REASON

(5) PROTECT PEOPLE AND NATIONS
WITH FAIR LAWS AND JUST COURTS

(6) LET ALL NATIONS RULE INTERNALLY
RESOLVING EXTERNAL DISPUTES IN A
WORLD COURT

(7) AVOID PETTY LAWS AND USELESS
OFFICIALS

(8) BALANCE PERSONAL RIGHTS WITH
SOCIAL DUTIES

(9) PRIZE TRUTH — BEAUTY — LOVE —
SEEKING HARMONY WITH THE INFINITE

(10) BE NOT A CANCER ON THE EARTH —
LEAVE ROOM FOR NATURE —
LEAVE ROOM FOR NATURE

The 4 shorter messages that appear on the four vertical surfaces of the capstone are also in a different language. The explanatory tablet near the Guidestones identifies these languages as Babylonian Cuneiform (north), Classical Greek (east), Sanskrit (south), and Egyptian Hieroglyphs (west). It provides what is presumably an English translation that states, "Let these be guidestones to an age of reason."

It states the astrological features as:

(1) CHANNEL THROUGH STONE INDICATES CELESTIAL POLE

(2) HORIZONTAL SLOT INDICATES ANNUAL TRAVEL OF SUN

(3) SUNBEAM THROUGH CAPSTONE MARKS NOONTIME THROUGHOUT THE YEAR

The time capsule inscription reads:

PLACED SIX FEET BELOW THIS SPOT
ON (left blank)
TO BE OPENED ON (left blank)

After any of these global events, even some of the largest of these cities would be lost. If they were not immediately disintegrated, they would be completely covered over in just a few hundred years. After a few thousand years, there would be nothing left but the concrete, and because of the way modern concrete was made, it would be completely gone by around ten Thousand years. We really would have no ideal what was once here. All of the ancient structures that still remain, were all built by cutting solid block.

By using solid blocks, they could remain almost indefinitely. If preserved in the right location, for any length of time, we could have no ideal how long one of these structures may have actually been here. A good example of an out of place construction that was built by this type of solid block is located in the jungles of Cambodia. There they have temples that are said to have been built by the Khmer civilization as early as the eighth century AD. On a temple known as Ta Prohm, there are hundreds of stone circles surrounding animals that were very familiar in my time.

Almost every square inch is covered with some kind of depiction, such as monkeys, deer, water buffalo, parrots, swans and lizards. The most unique of all of these is what appears to be a stegosaurus, a dinosaur that was supposed to have roamed the earth during the Jurassic period approximately 200 million to 145 million years ago. The site was so unique that it earned a spot in the first Laura Croft movie. Some of its construction resembles that of Tiahuanaco, near Lake Titicaca in Bolivia, Bolivia is around the world from Cambodia.

Another good example of something strange happened on February 13, 1961, while Wallace Lane, Virginia Maxey, and Mike Mikesell were seeking mineral specimens for their "LM & V Rockhounds Gem and Gift Shop" in Olancha, California. In a statement made by Maxey, he stated, "We hiked about three miles north, after we had parked some five miles east of State Highway 395, south of Olancha, California." They claimed that around lunchtime, all three placed their specimens in the rock sack Mikesell was carrying, and the next day in the gift shop's workroom, they began to cut them open. While cutting what he thought was a geode, he found a perfectly circular section of an extremely hard, white material, which looked very similar to porcelain.

In the center of its cylinder was a 2-millimeter shaft of bright metal that responded to a magnet. The outer layer was encrusted with fossil shells, and two nonmagnetic metallic metal objects that resembled a nail and a washer. Within the inner layer, a layer of decomposing copper surrounded the porcelain cylinder. According to discoverer Virginia Maxey, a geologist she spoke with told her the nodule had taken at least 500,000 years to form. Creationist, Ron Calais, took photographs of the nodule in both X ray, and natural light. The X-ray of the upper end of the object revealed some sort of tiny spring or helix. INFO Journal Publisher Ronald J. Willis stated that it could actually be "the remains of a corroded piece of metal with threads."

In a speech by HRH The Prince of Wales titled "Less Than 100 Months to Act", 12th March 2009, it stated, " As I know you well understand, the race in which we are all engaged now is to restore harmony to the forces of Nature unleashed by climate change and so ensure our very ability to survive because, ladies and gentlemen, any difficulties which the world faces today will be as nothing compared to the full effects which global warming will have on the world-wide economy. It will result in vast movements of people escaping either flooding or droughts; in uncertain production of food and lack of water and, of course, increasing social instability and potential conflict. In other words, it will affect the well-being of every man, woman and child on our planet....The best projections tell us that we have less than one hundred months to alter our behaviour before we risk catastrophic climate change, and the unimaginable horrors that this would bring."

My conclusion of the information

is that at an unknown time in history, it was figured out by using basic astrological observations and mathematical principles that the planet was not a very safe place to live. Not only because of horrifying events that seemed to reoccur over long periods of time, but also because every year the planet was getting closer and closer to the sun, and every year the planet was getting warmer and warmer. It was indisputable that eventually this would lead to the depletion of the atmosphere, exposing the people to more and more of the suns blinding rays and radiation, inevitably changing things like hair color, eye sight, eye structure and eye color. It was believed that because of the affect this would have on the presence of the pigment melanin, that our skin would eventually become darker and darker, drier and drier, until it would lead to the death of the entire race.

It was decided that a plan would have to be put in place, a plan which would help only the most important of this race to survive. This plan was to be handed down from generation to generation, carried out unnoticed as the rest of the planet continued with their daily duties as if nothing was ever going to change. It was believed if the population was informed of these coming events, they would work to help their own families, and that this would leave no one to help them.

It was decided that the blame would be put on something that they would call global warming. This was done not only because it was thought it would shift the blame toward the people, but also to give them a better chance for survival. It would give them more time for the building of the underground cities for the future purpose of keeping the important people away from the exposure of too much sun, heat and radiation. With this plan in place, they could use the common people as slaves in order to help this elite group to survive the reoccurring disasters and the horrifyingly inevitable ends.

Only a select few would be the builders of these underground cities, and they would not be given the true purpose behind why they were being built, but instead a false belief of war would be implied, if they were given any thought at all. In time, with this plan in place, only the common people would be exposed to the suns rays and intense heat. And if everything went as planned, they would have no idea that they were considered the unworthy, the weak. They would simply just work their lives away, never knowing that their descendants were to be left behind to die on this dieing planet, thought of as nothing more than the meek left to inherit it as the elite moved to the next one.

To prepare for the arrival of the people of the underground cities onto the surface of the next planet, large sources of water would have to be located. This was to be accomplished by using unwanted people, crazy people that nobody would miss. These people were to be dropped off, with chips implanted in their bodies so that they could not only be tracked to see how long they could survive, but where they would gather in order to detect where they were finding water, food, etc. By using these people, they would be able to insure that if anything at all went wrong, nobody would believe anything that they had to say.

Another source of slave labor was prisoners, many were unwanted as well, nobody would miss them, and they had already been used to make many cities in the past that were once considered prisons for the people. The difference was, by the time these elite were to be prepared for the journey to the new world, the slaves on the surface would be almost completely black in color, their hair, their eyes, and their skin. It was thought that this exposure would make their skin so dark, and so dry, that it would be almost scaly. When added to the tunnel diggers distorted eyes, they would resemble serpents or snakes. After some debate, it was decided that they would call this new world, earth.

NEW WORLD BIBLE